LOW CALORIE HIGH PROTEIN

Healthy Eating Made Easy: A Beginner's Guide to Low-Calorie, High-Protein Meal Prep Recipes for Weight Loss and Optimal Health!

Meal Prep CookBook

Theresa Lynch

Table of Content

Pho-Inspired Beef Noodle Soup
Pork & Pineapple Tacos
Baked Fish & Kale Lavash Wraps
Easy Sesame Chicken with Green Beans
Pita Panzanella Salad with Meatballs
Coconut Curry Shrimp
Cilantro-Lime Chicken Tacos
Grilled Flank Steak with Tomato Salad
Chicken & Zucchini Casserole
Egg Roll-Inspired Cabbage Rolls
Easy Shrimp Tacos
Quinoa-Stuffed Peppers
Instant-Pot Sausage & Peppers
Chicken Cutlets with Creamy Spinach & Roasted
Red Pepper Sauce
Spicy Noodles with Pork, Scallions & Bok Choy
Shrimp Cauliflower Fried Rice
Shepherd's Pie with Cauliflower Topping
Creamy Lemon Pasta with Shrimp
Spinach Ravioli with Artichokes & Olives
Lemon-Garlic Chicken with Green Beans
Polenta Bowls with Roasted Vegetables & Fried
Eggs
Salt & Vinegar Sheet-Pan Chicken & Brussels
Sprouts
Spicy Noodles with Pork, Scallions & Bok Choy
Honey-Garlic Chicken Thighs with Carrots &
Broccoli
Easy Spicy Salmon Cakes

Introduction

Welcome to the Low Calorie High Protein Meal Prep Recipe Cookbook!

Eating healthy doesn't have to be boring, and this book will help you make delicious and nutritious meals while keeping your calorie count low! Inside, you'll find a variety of recipes that offer a balance of low calories and high protein, perfect for anyone on a weight loss journey or looking to maintain a healthy lifestyle.

All of the recipes are easy to prepare and can be prepped for the week ahead, ensuring you get the most out of your meals. Whether you're a beginner or a seasoned pro at meal prepping, this cookbook has something for everyone. So, grab your apron and get ready to create some delicious and nutritious meals!

A low calorie high protein diet is a popular option for those looking to lose weight. This type of diet focuses on reducing the amount of calories consumed while increasing the amount of protein. This helps to keep hunger at bay and increases the body's ability to burn fat for energy.

When following a low calorie high protein diet, it is important to focus on eating healthy, whole foods. This means avoiding processed foods, refined sugars, and unhealthy fats. Instead, focus on eating lean proteins like fish, chicken, and tofu, as well as high-fiber fruits and vegetables. It is also important to include healthy fats like avocado, nuts, and seeds in your diet to help keep you satiated and your energy levels up.

In order to get the most out of this diet, it is important to plan your meals in advance. This will help you avoid unhealthy snacking and ensure that you are getting the right balance of nutrients. Aim to eat several small meals throughout the day, including a protein-rich breakfast, lunch, and dinner. Snacks should also include protein, such as a handful of nuts or a hard-boiled egg.

It is also important to stay hydrated when following a low calorie high protein diet. Water helps to keep your body functioning properly and helps to flush out toxins. Aim to drink at least 8 glasses of water each day.

Finally, it is important to remember to be patient. Weight loss is a gradual process and it can take some time to see results. However, if you stick to a healthy diet and exercise regularly, you should see results in no time.

Low Calorie High Protein Recipes

Creamy Chicken, Brussels Sprouts & Mushrooms One-Pot Pasta

Servings : 5

27 grams Protein

41.7 grams Carb

10.3 grams Fat

353 Cal Per Serving

Est. Active Time: 35 mins

Est. Total Time: 40 mins

Ingredients

- 8 ounces whole-wheat linguine or spaghetti
- 1 pound boneless, skinless chicken thighs
- 4 cups sliced mushrooms
- 2 cups sliced Brussels sprouts
- 1 medium onion, chopped
- 4 cloves garlic, thinly sliced
- 2 tablespoons Boursin cheese

- 1 ¼ teaspoons dried thyme
- ¾ teaspoon dried rosemary
- ¾ teaspoon salt
- 4 cups water
- 2 tablespoons chopped fresh chives

Instructions

- In a sizable pot, combine the pasta, chicken, mushrooms, Brussels sprouts, onion, garlic, Boursin cheese, thyme, and salt. Stir in the water.
- Using a high heat, bring to a boil. Boil for 10 to 12 minutes, stirring periodically, until the pasta is tender and the water has nearly completely evaporated.
- With occasional stirring, remove from heat and allow to stand for 5 minutes.
- Serve with chives added.

Creamy Skillet Ranch Chicken & Broccoli

Servings : 4

29 grams Protein

6 grams Carb

26 grams Fat

374 Cal Per Serving

Est. Active Time: 30 mins

Est. Total Time: 30 mins

Ingredients

- 1 pound of peeled, chopped, and boneless, skinless chicken breast
- ½ teaspoon of salt, divided
- 12 teaspoon split powdered pepper plus more for garnish
- 2 tablespoons of extra virgin olive oil, divided
- 4 cups broccoli florets, chopped
- 2 tablespoons water
- 1.5 cups thick cream

- White wine vinegar, 2 teaspoons
- 2 tablespoons of mayo
- 1 teaspoon cornstarch
- 1/2 tsp. of onion powder
- 1/2 tsp. of garlic powder
- 14 cup chopped fresh herb mixture (chives, dill, tarragon, basil)

Instructions

- Add 1/4 teaspoons of salt and pepper to the chicken.
- In a big skillet, heat 1 tablespoon of oil over medium heat. Add the chicken and cook, tossing occasionally, for 5 to 7 minutes, or until the chicken is browned and barely cooked through. Place on a platter.
- Broccoli, water, and the final tablespoon of oil go into the pan. Cook under a cover for 3 to 4 minutes, stirring periodically,

or until tender-crisp. Place on the same platter as the chicken.

- In a measuring cup, combine the remaining 1/4 teaspoon each of salt and pepper with the cream, vinegar, mayonnaise, cornstarch, onion powder, and garlic powder. Pour the cream mixture into the pan and raise the heat to medium-high. Bring to a simmer and cook for two minutes while stirring until thickened.
- Herbs should be added to the pan along with the chicken and broccoli, and the mixture should be cooked for an additional 1 to 2 minutes while stirring.
- If desired, add pepper as a garnish.

Ginger-Orange Chicken Thighs with Baby Bok Choy

Servings : 4

30 grams Protein

18 grams Carb

11.1 grams Fat

299 Cal Per Serving

Est. Active Time: 40 mins

Est. Total Time: 40 mins

Ingredients

- 2 pounds bone-in chicken thighs
- ½ teaspoon Chinese five-spice powder
- ¼ teaspoon salt
- 2 teaspoons peanut oil
- 1 ½ pounds baby bok choy, halved
- 1 (11 ounce) can mandarin oranges in light syrup, drained
- 2 tablespoons reduced-sodium tamari
- 2 tablespoons Shaoxing rice wine or dry sherry, divided

- 2 tablespoons minced shallot
- 1 tablespoon grated garlic
- 1 tablespoon grated fresh ginger
- 1 ½ teaspoons cornstarch

Instructions

- Set the oven to 450 degrees Fahrenheit.
- After thoroughly drying the chicken, season with salt and five-spice powder. Over medium heat, warm oil in a sizable cast-iron or other ovenproof skillet. Add the chicken, skin-side down, and cook for 6 to 8 minutes, or until the skin is golden brown. Place the bok choy in the pan after flipping the chicken over.
- Place in the oven in the pan. Roast for about 15 minutes, or until an instant-read thermometer that is put into a thigh without touching the bone reads 165 degrees F.

- Add 1/4 cup of mandarin orange syrup to a small pot in the meanwhile. (Drain the leftover syrup, saving the oranges.) Add shallot, garlic, ginger, 1 tablespoon rice wine (or sherry), and tamari to the pan.
- Cook for three minutes at a simmer over medium heat. In a small bowl, combine the cornstarch and remaining 1 tablespoon rice wine (or sherry); whisk to combine well before adding to the sauce. For about a minute, while stirring, cook the sauce until it thickens. Pour the sauce through a strainer into a heatproof measuring cup or bowl, then add the oranges you set aside.
- Serve the sauce on top of the chicken and bok choy.

Spicy Slow-Cooker Chicken with Lime, Basil & Mint

Servings : 12

24.3 grams Protein

7.8 grams Carb

3 grams Fat

157 Cal Per Serving

Est. Active Time: 30 mins

Est. Total Time: 3 hrs 30 mins

Ingredients

- 3 cups low-sodium chicken broth
- 3 shallots, very thinly sliced
- ¼ cup fish sauce
- 2 tablespoons packed light brown sugar
- 2-4 Thai chiles, very thinly sliced, or 1 teaspoon crushed red pepper
- 2 teaspoons lime zest
- 4 pounds skin-on, bone-in chicken breasts
- 2 cups julienned or grated carrots

- ½ cup lime juice
- ⅓ cup sliced fresh mint
- ⅓ cup sliced fresh basil

Instructions

- In a 6-quart slow cooker, mix the broth, shallots, fish sauce, brown sugar, chilies (or crushed red pepper), and lime zest. Place the chicken in the broth with the meat side up. Cook for three hours on high or six hours on low.
- Place the chicken on a fresh cutting board after removal. Shred the meat and discard the skin. Add the carrots, lime juice, mint, and basil to the slow cooker before adding the chicken back in.

Oven-Baked Salmon with Charred Onions & Old Bay Radishes

Servings : 4

29.1 grams Protein

7.4 grams Carb

19.3 grams Fat

324 Cal Per Serving

Est. Active Time: 30 mins

Est. Total Time: 45 mins

Ingredients

- 2 medium onions, sliced 1/2 inch thick
- 4 tablespoons extra-virgin olive oil, divided
- Zest of 2 lemons
- 1 ½ teaspoons cracked pepper
- 1 teaspoon kosher salt, divided
- 4 (5 ounce) skin-on salmon filets
- 6 large radishes, cut into wedges, plus more thinly sliced for garnish
- 1 teaspoon Old Bay seasoning

- ½ teaspoon sugar
- Fresh cilantro & flaky sea salt for garnish

Instructions

- Set the oven to 325 degrees Fahrenheit.
- Ensure that a sizable cast-iron skillet is hot. Onions should be added and cooked for 10 to 15 minutes, occasionally pressing down, until totally browned on one side. Turn the food over and cook for a further 8 to 10 minutes, pressing down occasionally, until the second side is blackened. Place in a large basin and tightly cover. Steam for fifteen minutes.
- In the meantime, combine 1/2 teaspoon salt, 1/2 teaspoon pepper, and 2 tablespoons oil in a small bowl. Salmon should be placed skin-side down in a medium ovenproof nonstick or cast-iron skillet with 1 tablespoon oil. Apply the

salmon with the lemon zest mixture. Bake for 14 to 16 minutes, or until barely heated through. Water in a small pan is brought to a boil.

- Add the radish wedges and simmer for 5 to 6 minutes, or until barely tender. Drain and pat dry. Dry the pan before adding Old Bay and the final tablespoon of oil. For about a minute, heat over medium-low until sizzling. The radish wedges are added after the heat has turned off. Cover up to stay warm.

- In a food processor, combine the onions, the remaining 1/2 teaspoon of salt, and the sugar. Puree until completely smooth.

- Along with the onion purée and radishes, serve the salmon. If desired, garnish with chopped cilantro and flaky salt.

Slow-Cooker Braised Beef with Carrots & Turnips

Servings : 8

34.7 grams Protein

12.8 grams Carb

10.7 grams Fat

318 Cal Per Serving

Est. Active Time: 40 mins

Est. Total Time: 4 hrs

Ingredients

- 1 tablespoon kosher salt
- 2 teaspoons ground cinnamon
- ½ teaspoon ground allspice
- ½ teaspoon ground pepper
- ¼ teaspoon ground cloves
- 3-3 1/2 pounds beef chuck roast, trimmed
- 2 tablespoons extra-virgin olive oil
- 1 medium onion, chopped
- 3 cloves garlic, sliced

- 1 cup red wine
- 1 (28 ounce) can whole tomatoes, preferably San Marzano
- 5 medium carrots, cut into 1-inch pieces
- 2 medium turnips, peeled and cut into 1/2-inch pieces
- Chopped fresh basil for garnish

Instructions

- In a small bowl, mix the spices, cloves, pepper, cinnamon, salt, and allspice. All over the beef, rub the mixture.
- A big skillet with medium heat is used to heat the oil. Add the steak and heat for 4 to 5 minutes on each side, or until browned. To a 5- to 6-quart slow cooker, transfer.
- To the pan, add the onion and garlic. Cook for two minutes while stirring. Wine and tomatoes (along with their

juice) should be added. Bring to a boil while breaking up the tomatoes and scraping up any browned bits. Carrots and turnips should be added to the slow cooker along with the mixture.

- Cook on High for 4 hours or Low for 8 hours with the cover on.
- Slice the beef after removing it from the slow cooker. Serve the beef with the sauce, veggies, and basil on the side.

Green Chicken Curry

Servings : 4

24.3 grams Protein

20.4 grams Carb

20.3 grams Fat

360 Cal Per Serving

Est. Active Time: …mins

Est. Total Time: 40 mins

Ingredients

- 2 tablespoons canola oil
- 1 pound boneless, skinless chicken thighs, trimmed, cut into bite-size pieces
- 1 bunch scallions, sliced
- 1 medium sweet potato, cut into 1/2-inch cubes
- 1 14-ounce can "lite" coconut milk
- 2 tablespoons Thai green, red or yellow curry paste
- 1 tablespoon fish sauce

- 3 cups sliced bok choy
- 1 ½ cups halved green beans, fresh or frozen (thawed)
- ¼ cup chopped fresh basil
- 1 tablespoon lime juice

Instructions

- In a sizable skillet, heat the oil over medium-high heat. Cook, tossing the chicken and scallions for 4 to 5 minutes, or until the chicken is no longer pink. Make use of a slotted spoon to transfer to a dish.
- Cook the sweet potato in the pan for two minutes while stirring.
- Bring to a simmer after adding the coconut milk, curry paste, fish sauce, bok choy, and green beans. Reduce the heat to medium, cover the pan, and simmer

the vegetables for 5 to 7 minutes, stirring occasionally.

- Once heated through, add the chicken and any remaining liquids to the pan and cook for an additional 2 minutes. Remove from heat and toss in lime juice and basil.

Packet Baked Tuna Steaks & Vegetables with Creamy Dijon-Turmeric Sauce

Servings : 4

36.4 grams Protein

14 grams Carb

11.3 grams Fat

312 Cal Per Serving

Est. Active Time: 20 mins

Est. Total Time: 30 mins

Ingredients

- ¼ cup mayonnaise
- 1 tablespoon chopped fresh parsley
- 2 teaspoons Dijon mustard
- 1 teaspoon honey
- ½ teaspoon ground turmeric
- 2 cups thinly sliced Yukon Gold potatoes (about 1/8-inch)
- ½ teaspoon salt, divided
- ⅛ teaspoon ground pepper, plus 1/4 teaspoon, divided

- 4 cups chopped kale
- 1 ¼ pounds tuna (about 1 inch thick), cut into 4 pieces

Instructions

- Set the oven to 450 degrees Fahrenheit. Cut four big parchment paper sheets, each measuring about 16 by 12 inches (or use pre-cut parchment sheets).
- In a small bowl, mix the mayonnaise, parsley, mustard, honey, and turmeric.
- The long sides of the parchment sheets should be closest to you when placing them on a work area to create packets. Each should be opened after being folded in half (short sides together). Sprinkle 1/4 teaspoon salt and 1/8 teaspoon pepper over the side of each sheet of parchment that has 1/2 cup of potatoes. Add a piece of tuna and one cup of kale to

the top of each. Add the remaining 1/4 teaspoon of salt and pepper to the tuna. Apply the mayonnaise mixture on the brush.

- Close the sachets and use small, precise folds to seal the edges. On a sizable baking sheet, arrange the packages.
- Bake for 10 to 15 minutes, or until the fish is barely cooked through. (Caution: steam may be present while opening one package carefully to check for doneness.)
- Place each packet on a separate plate. Observe for three minutes. Use scissors to make an X in the top of each packet, then carefully fold it open to use.

Chicken Parmesan Pizza

Servings : 5

27.7 grams Protein

41 grams Carb

12.5 grams Fat

373 Cal Per Serving

Est. Active Time: 20 mins

Est. Total Time: 40 mins

Ingredients

- 1 pound whole-wheat pizza dough
- 1 ½ cups shredded cooked chicken breast (8 ounces)
- ¾ cup pizza sauce, divided
- ¼ teaspoon garlic powder
- ¼ teaspoon crushed red pepper
- All-purpose flour for rolling dough
- 1 cup shredded low-fat mozzarella cheese or 4 ounces fresh mozzarella, torn into pieces

- ½ cup grated Parmesan cheese, divided
- ¼ cup thinly sliced fresh basil

Instructions

- Set oven to 475 degrees Fahrenheit. Spray cooking oil on a sizable baking sheet with a rim. While you prepare the toppings, let the dough rest at room temperature.
- In a small bowl, combine chicken, 1/4 cup pizza sauce, garlic powder, and crushed red pepper.
- On a surface that has been lightly dusted with flour, roll out the pizza dough to roughly the size of the baking sheet. To the prepared baking sheet, transfer. Over the dough, smear the remaining 1/2 cup pizza sauce.
- Cover the sauce with the chicken mixture. Add 1/4 cup of Parmesan and mozzarella

on top. Bake for 16 to 20 minutes, or until bubbling and golden. Basil and the final 1/4 cup of Parmesan are added as garnish. 10 pieces should be cut.

Turkey & Sweet Potato Chili

Servings : 6

16.3 grams Protein

16.2 grams Carb

8.8 grams Fat

205 Cal Per Serving

Est. Active Time: 30 mins

Est. Total Time: 50 mins

Ingredients

- 1 tablespoon extra-virgin olive oil
- 1 pound ground turkey
- 1 large yellow onion, chopped
- 3 cloves garlic, minced
- 1 tablespoon minced seeded canned chipotle pepper in adobo sauce
- 1 (28 ounce) can no-salt-added diced tomatoes
- 2 medium sweet potatoes (about 5 oz. each), peeled and diced

- 2 cups unsalted chicken broth
- ¾ teaspoon salt
- 2 tablespoons lime juice
- Chopped avocado for garnish

Instructions

- Over medium-high heat, warm the oil in a big, heavy pot. Add the turkey and simmer for 5 minutes, stirring frequently to break up the meat.
- Add the onion and garlic; simmer for about 5 minutes, stirring frequently, until tender. Cook the chipotle for approximately a minute, stirring regularly, until fragrant. Add salt, broth, tomatoes, and sweet potatoes after stirring. Melt over medium-high heat, then simmer. Cover, lower the heat to medium, and boil the sweet potatoes for

about 20 minutes, or until they are fork-tender.

- Remove the lid; simmer the chili uncovered for a further 10 minutes, or to the desired consistency, while stirring regularly. Add lime juice and stir.
- Distribute the chili equally among 6 bowls and, if preferred, top with avocado.

Sheet-Pan Chicken Fajita Bowl

Servings : 4

42.7 grams Protein

23.2 grams Carb

9.9 grams Fat

343 Cal Per Serving

Est. Active Time: 20 mins

Est. Total Time: 40 mins

Ingredients

- 2 teaspoons chili powder
- 2 teaspoons ground cumin
- ¾ teaspoon salt, divided
- ½ teaspoon garlic powder
- ½ teaspoon smoked paprika
- ¼ teaspoon ground pepper
- 2 tablespoons olive oil, divided
- 1 ¼ pounds chicken tenders
- 1 medium yellow onion, sliced
- 1 medium red bell pepper, sliced

- 1 medium green bell pepper, sliced
- 4 cups chopped stemmed kale
- 1 (15 ounce) can no-salt-added black beans, rinsed
- ¼ cup low-fat plain Greek yogurt
- 1 tablespoon lime juice
- 2 teaspoons water

Instructions

- Preheat the oven to 425 degrees F and place a big rimmed baking sheet inside.
- In a sizable bowl, combine the chili powder, cumin, 1/2 teaspoon salt, garlic powder, paprika, and ground pepper. One teaspoon of the spice mixture should be added to a larger bowl and left aside. The remaining spice mixture in the big bowl should be incorporated with 1 Tbsp oil. Toss to coat the chicken, onion, and red and green bell peppers.

- When done baking, remove the pan and spray it with cooking spray. On the pan, distribute the chicken mixture in a uniform layer. For 15 minutes, roast.
- In the meantime, place the kale and black beans in a large bowl and add the remaining 1/4 teaspoon of salt and 1 tablespoon of olive oil. Toss to coat.
- Pan should be taken out of the oven.
- Chicken and veggies are stirred. Evenly distribute the greens and beans over top. Cook the chicken for an additional 5 to 7 minutes, or until it is well done.
- In the meantime, combine the saved spice combination with the yogurt, lime juice, and water.
- Four bowls should receive the chicken and veggie mixture. Serve after drizzling with the yogurt dressing.

Greek-Inspired Burgers with Herb-Feta Sauce

Servings : 4

29.8 grams Protein

23.5 grams Carb

18.1 grams Fat

375 Cal Per Serving

Est. Active Time: 25 mins

Est. Total Time: 25 mins

Ingredients

- 1 cup nonfat plain Greek yogurt
- ¼ cup crumbled feta cheese
- 3 tablespoons chopped fresh oregano, divided
- ¼ teaspoon lemon zest
- 2 teaspoons lemon juice
- ¾ teaspoon salt, divided
- 1 small red onion
- 1 pound ground lamb or ground beef
- ½ teaspoon ground peppe

- 2 whole-wheat pitas, halved, split and warmed
- 1 cup sliced cucumber
- 1 plum tomato, sliced

Instructions

- Broiler or grill should be preheated to high.
- In a small bowl, combine yogurt, feta, 1 tablespoon oregano, lemon zest, lemon juice, and 1/4 teaspoon salt.
- To create 1/4 cup, slice an onion into 1/4-inch-thick slices. To create 1/4 cup, add extra onion and finely chop. (Save any leftover onions for a different use.) The remaining 2 tablespoons of oregano, together with 1/2 teaspoons of salt and pepper, are combined with the meat and chopped onion in a large bowl. 4 by 3

inch oval patties made from the mixture should be formed.

- Burgers should be grilled or broiled for 4 to 6 minutes per side, flipping once, until an instant-read thermometer reads 160 degrees F. Serve the sauce, onion slices, cucumber, and tomato in pita half sandwiches.

Coconut-Curry Cod Stew with Sweet Potato & Rice

Servings : 4

19.2 grams Protein

49.5 grams Carb

11.3 grams Fat

382 Cal Per Serving

Est. Active Time: 30 mins

Est. Total Time: 40 mins

Ingredients

- 2 cups water
- ¾ cup long-grain brown ric
- 1 tablespoon canola oil
- 1 tablespoon chopped fresh ginger
- 1 tablespoon chopped garlic
- 1 yellow bell pepper, halved, seeded, and sliced
- 1 pound sweet potatoes (about 2 small or 1 large), peeled and cut into 1 1/2-inch pieces

- 1 tablespoon curry powder
- ½ teaspoon salt
- 1 (15 ounce) can light coconut milk
- 4 cod fillets (4-5 oz. each)
- 3 tablespoons chopped fresh cilantro, plus more for garnish
- 2 teaspoons lime juice

Instructions

- In a medium saucepan, combine the water and rice. Bring to a boil. Reduce heat, cover, and simmer for about 40 minutes, or until the rice is cooked and most of the water has been absorbed. Whenever required, drain any extra water.
- In the interim, warm the oil in a big skillet over medium heat. Add the ginger and garlic, and stir-fry for 30 seconds or so, until fragrant. Stir in the salt, curry

powder, bell pepper, and sweet potatoes to thoroughly coat everything. Simmer after adding coconut milk. For 10 to 15 minutes, or until the sweet potatoes are barely cooked when pierced with a fork, cover and boil, stirring periodically.

- Place the cod fillets in the pan, cover it, and cook for an additional 5 to 8 minutes, or until the sweet potatoes are tender and the fish flakes easily when tested with a fork.

- Add cilantro and lime juice, stirring slowly. Over rice, serve the stew. If desired, add more cilantro as a garnish.

Instant Pot Beef Bourguignon

Servings : 8

24 grams Protein

14.9 grams Carb

9.4 grams Fat

252 Cal Per Serving

Est. Active Time: 60 mins

Est. Total Time: 9" mins

Ingredients

- 1 ¾ pounds beef stew meat, preferably chuck, trimmed and cut into 1 1/4-inch chunks
- ¾ teaspoon salt, divided
- ½ teaspoon ground pepper
- 8 teaspoons canola oil, divided
- ⅔ cup dry red wine
- 1 large onion, chopped (1 1/2 cups)
- 1 cup diced carrots (2 medium)
- 4 cloves garlic, minced

- ¾ teaspoon dried thyme leaves
- 1 (15 ounce) can no-salt-added diced tomatoes
- 1 cup low-sodium beef broth
- 1 bay leaf
- 1 pound cremini or button mushrooms, quartered (5 cups)
- 2 cups frozen pearl onions (8 oz.)
- 2 tablespoons cornstarch
- 2 tablespoons water
- 1-2 teaspoons red-wine or cider vinegar
- 2 tablespoons chopped fresh parsley for garnish

Instructions

- Dry off the beef and season with 1/2 tsp. salt and pepper. In a big, heavy skillet over medium-high heat, warm 2 tablespoons of oil. Add half the beef and cook, stirring periodically, for 4 to 6 minutes, or until nicely browned. Place on a platter. The remaining steak is browned in 2 teaspoons of oil and then transferred to a plate. Add the wine and simmer for 1 to 2 minutes, scraping off any browned parts as you go.

- In the meantime, use the Saute option on a multicooker to warm 2 teaspoons of oil. Add the chopped onion and carrots; simmer for 4 to 6 minutes, stirring periodically, until tender.

- Add the garlic and thyme, and stir-fry for 30 to 60 seconds or until fragrant. Add the steak, any accumulated juices, the reduced wine, tomatoes, broth, and bay leaf.

-

- Twist the steam-release handle to the sealed position after locking the lid in place. Choose Pressure Cook/High for 40 minutes (or pressure-cook for 40 minutes according to the manufacturer's instructions). Allow the pressure to naturally release for 15 minutes after the pressure cooking is finished.

-

- In the meantime, preheat the skillet with the remaining 2 teaspoons of oil over medium-high heat. Add the mushrooms and the final 1/4 tsp of salt. Cook, stirring occasionally, for 8 to 10 minutes, or until the mushrooms are tender and lightly browned. Cook pearl onions according to package directions; drain.

- Manually release any leftover pressure in the pressure cooker. Choose the Saute option. In a small basin, combine cornstarch and water; add to the stew. Cook for about 2 minutes while stirring to slightly thicken the mixture. Add the pearl onions and mushrooms to the vinegar and stir to combine. If desired, add parsley as a garnish.

Mushroom-Swiss Turkey Burgers

Servings : 1

33.5 grams Protein

10.3 grams Carb

18.4 grams Fat

332 Cal Per Serving

Est. Active Time: 20 mins

Est. Total Time: 30 mins

Ingredients

- 2 tablespoons extra-virgin olive oil
- 1 clove garlic, minced
- ¾ teaspoon ground pepper, divided
- ½ teaspoon salt, divided
- 8 portobello mushroom caps, stems and gills removed
- 1 pound lean ground turkey
- 2 teaspoons gluten-free Worcestershire sauce
- 1 teaspoon Dijon mustard

- 4 slices Swiss cheese
- 1 small tomato, thinly sliced
- 3 cups baby arugula

Instructions

- Set the grill to medium-high heat (400-450 degrees F). In a small bowl, mix the oil, garlic, and 1/4 teaspoon of salt and pepper. Portobello mushroom caps should be brushed with the oil mixture and let to marinade for 10 minutes at room temperature.
- In the meantime, add the remaining 1/4 teaspoon salt, 1/2 teaspoon pepper, Worcestershire, and mustard in a medium bowl. Mix slowly to incorporate. (Avoid overmixing.) Four 3/4-inch-thick patties should be formed; set aside.
- the grill rack with oil. Place the mushrooms on the oiled grill rack with

the caps facing up. Grill, covered, for 4 minutes per side, or until just tender. Place the mushrooms on a platter and cover to maintain warmth. Place the turkey patties on the rack after re-oiling it.

- Cook the patties for 4 to 5 minutes on each side, covered, until they are just beginning to brown and an instant-read thermometer placed in the center reads 165 degrees F. During the final minute of cooking, top each patty with 1 piece of cheese. Place the patties on a platter and give them time to rest for five minutes. (If your grill is big enough, grill the patties and portobello mushrooms simultaneously.)
- Each patty should be placed on the portobello cap's stem side. Distribute the tomato and arugula slices on top evenly.

Serve right away and top with the remaining portobello caps, stem-side down.

Spice-Seared Salmon with Greek-Style Green Beans

Servings : 4

29 grams Protein

16 grams Carb

15 grams Fat

311 Cal Per Serving

Est. Active Time: 25 mins

Est. Total Time: 35 mins

Ingredients

- 2 tablespoons olive oil, divided
- 1 small yellow onion, diced
- 4 cloves garlic, chopped
- 1 (15 ounce) can no-salt-added diced tomatoes
- 2 tablespoons chopped fresh dill, divided
- ½ teaspoon salt, divided
- 12 ounces green beans, stem ends trimmed (4 cups)
- ¼ cup lemon juice

- 1 pound salmon fillet with skin, cut into 4 portions
- 1 tablespoon Baharat Spice Mix
-

Instructions

- Set the oven to 425 degrees Fahrenheit. Cooking spray should be used to line a large baking sheet with a rim with parchment paper or foil.
- In a big saucepan, heat 1 tablespoon of oil to medium-high heat. Add the onion and stir often for 3 to 5 minutes, or until transparent. Garlic is added and cooked for one minute. Add tomatoes, 1 Tbsp. dill, and 1/4 tsp. salt; stir well. Heat to a boil. Add green beans and stir. Turn down the heat to low, cover the pot, and cook the beans for 10 to 15 minutes, stirring occasionally.

- In the meantime, combine lemon juice with the final tablespoon of oil in a small bowl. Salmon should be coated well with the lemon-oil combination. On the prepared baking sheet, lay the salmon skin-side down.
- Sprinkle remaining 1/4 tsp. salt along with the spice mixture. For about 10 minutes, roast the salmon until the middle is barely opaque.
- Place a piece of salmon on each plate, then divide the green bean mixture among them and top with the final 1 Tbsp. of dill.

Coconut-Curry Chicken Cutlets

Servings : 4

31.7 grams Protein

27.2 grams Carb

16.7 grams Fat

387 Cal Per Serving

Est. Active Time: 20 mins

Est. Total Time: 20 mins

Ingredients

- 2 tablespoons grapeseed oil, divided
- 1 pound chicken cutlets
- 1 (14 ounce) can light coconut milk
- 1 tablespoon brown sugar
- 1 tablespoon red Thai curry paste
- 1 tablespoon lime juice
- 2 cups cooked quinoa
- Chopped fresh cilantro for garnish

Instructions

- In a large skillet over medium-high heat, warm 1 tablespoon of oil. If required, add the chicken in batches and cook, flipping once, for 1 to 3 minutes per side, until browned and cooked through. Place on a platter.
- Take the pan off the heat. In the pan, combine the remaining 1 tablespoon of oil with the coconut milk, brown sugar, curry powder, and lime juice. Cook for 5 to 10 minutes over high heat, stirring regularly, until the mixture is reduced by half. If preferred, top the chicken with cilantro before serving it with the grains and sauce.

Pho-Inspired Beef Noodle Soup

Servings : 4

30 grams Protein

33 grams Carb

6 grams Fat

306 Cal Per Serving

Est. Active Time: 30 mins

Est. Total Time: 40 mins

Ingredients

- 1 teaspoon canola oi
- 3 cloves garlic, minced
- 1 tablespoon minced fresh ginger
- 1 teaspoon ground pepper
- ¼ teaspoon ground cinnamon
- ¼ teaspoon ground cloves
- 4 cups unsalted beef broth
- 1 tablespoon fish sauce
- 4 ounces pad thai rice noodles
- 2 cups halved snap peas

- 1 cup thinly sliced white onion
- 1 pound beef sirloin, thinly sliced
- 1 cup bean sprouts
- ½ cup thinly sliced scallions (4 medium)
- ¼ cup thinly sliced fresh basil
- ¼ cup thinly sliced chile peppers, such as serrano or jalapeño
- Lime wedges for serving

Instructions

- Oil in a big pot is heated at a medium heat. Cook for one minute after adding the garlic, ginger, pepper, cinnamon, and cloves. Add fish sauce and broth after stirring, and heat to a boil. Simmer for 15 minutes with a partially covered pot over medium heat.
- Noodles should be prepared as directed on the package in the interim. Divide among 4 bowls after draining.

- Add beef, onion, and snap peas to the broth. After approximately a minute of simmering, the meat should be barely done; turn off the heat.
- Over the noodles, ladle the soup. Distribute the chilies, basil, scallions, and bean sprouts among the bowls. slices of lime are optional.

Pork & Pineapple Tacos

Servings : 6

35 grams Protein

31 grams Carb

5 grams Fat

306 Cal Per Serving

Est. Active Time: 30 mins

Est. Total Time: 7hrs 30 mins

Ingredients

- 1 tablespoon chili powder
- 2 teaspoons smoked paprika
- 1 teaspoon packed light brown suga
- ¾ teaspoon salt, divided
- ½ teaspoon garlic powder
- ½ teaspoon ground pepper
- 1 (2 pound) pork loin roast, trimmed
- ⅓ cup apple juice
- ½ cup lime juice

- 2 cups finely diced fresh pineapple (about 1/2 small pineapple)
- 1 cup finely diced seeded cucumber
- ¼ cup finely diced red onion
- 2 tablespoons cider vinegar
- 12 6-inch corn tortillas, warmed
- 2 cups shredded red cabbage

Instructions

- In a small bowl, mix the chili powder, paprika, brown sugar, pepper, 1/2 teaspoon salt, and garlic powder.
- In a 5- to 6-quart slow cooker, put the meat. Rub the pork with the spice mixture all over. Give the pork some apple juice to drink. Cook the pork on Low for 6 to 7 hours, covered, until it is tender to the fork.
- In the meantime, mix the lime juice with the final 1/4 tsp. of salt in a medium

bowl. Toss in the pineapple, cucumber, and onion after adding them. Keep chilled until you're ready to serve.

- Remove any discernible fat from the slow cooker's liquid. Shred the meat with two forks. Add vinegar and stir.
- Put a generous 1/4 cup of pulled pork and a drizzle of the cooking liquid on each tortilla before assembling the tacos.
- Add about 3 Tbsp. of the pineapple salsa on top, followed by about 2 1/2 Tbsp. of the chopped cabbage.

Baked Fish & Kale Lavash Wraps

Servings : 4

24.3 grams Protein

45.7 grams Carb

9.5 grams Fat

392 Cal Per Serving

Est. Active Time: 25 mins

Est. Total Time: 45 mins

Ingredients

- 5 ounces baby kale or baby spinach
- 3 tablespoons coarsely chopped fresh tarragon and/or dill
- 2 tablespoons finely chopped scallions
- ½ teaspoon kosher salt, divided
- ⅛ teaspoon plus 1/4 teaspoon ground pepper, divided
- 1 pound cod, halibut or barramundi, skinned and cut into 4 portions
- 4 sheets lavash

- 6 teaspoons extra-virgin olive oil, divided
- ¼ cup Very Versatile Roasted Red Pepper Sauce , plus more for serving

Instructions

- Set the oven to 375 degrees Fahrenheit. Cooking spray should be applied after lining a baking sheet with parchment paper. Start a kettle of water heating up.
- In a bowl, place the greens. For around five minutes, cover with boiling water and allow to wilt. Squeeze out extra moisture after draining it. Chop, then add back to the bowl. Add the scallions, tarragon (and/or dill), 1/4 teaspoon salt, and 1/8 teaspoon pepper.
- Dry the fish with paper towels before adding the final quarter teaspoon of salt and pepper.

- A lavash sheet should be placed on your work surface with the short side facing you in order to create each wrap. Place a piece of fish about 2 inches from the bottom edge and brush with 1 teaspoon oil.

- Place one-fourth of the greens on top of the fish after spreading one tablespoon of red pepper sauce on it. Place the burrito-style roll seam-side down on the heated pan. Brush the remaining 2 teaspoons of oil onto the wraps.

- Bake for 20 to 30 minutes, turning the pan from back to front halfway through, until the lavash is golden and crisp. Serve right away with more sauce if desired.

Easy Sesame Chicken with Green Beans

Servings : 4

23 grams Protein

12 grams Carb

13 grams Fat

257 Cal Per Serving

Est. Active Time: 25 mins

Est. Total Time: 35 mins

Ingredients

- 4 medium bone-in chicken thighs (about 5 oz. each), skin removed
- 4 teaspoons toasted sesame oil or canola oil, divided
- ¾ teaspoon garlic powder, divided
- ¼ teaspoon salt, divided
- 12 ounces green beans, trimmed
- 3 tablespoons hoisin sauce
- 1 tablespoon sesame seeds, toasted
- 1 medium scallion, chopped

Instructions

- Set the oven to 425 degrees Fahrenheit. Put the chicken on a big baking sheet with a rim. 1 teaspoon of oil should be used, along with 1/2 teaspoon of garlic powder and 1/8 teaspoon of salt. For 15 minutes, roast.

- Green beans should be mixed in a big bowl with the remaining 3 tsp of oil, 1/4 tsp of garlic powder, and 1/8 tsp of salt in the meantime.

- Add the beans to the baking sheet in an equal layer all the way around the chicken after it has been roasting for 15 minutes. Hoisin sauce should be applied to the chicken. Return to the oven and roast for an additional 10 to 15 minutes, or until the beans are soft and starting to brown and an instant-read thermometer inserted in the thickest part of the chicken without touching the bone reads 165 degrees F.

- In a small bowl, mix the sesame seeds and scallion. Sprinkle the remaining sesame seed mixture over the chicken and toss the remaining half of the sesame seed mixture with the beans.

Pita Panzanella Salad with Meatballs

Servings : 6

34 grams Protein

30 grams Carb

15 grams Fat

380 Cal Per Serving

Est. Active Time: 50 mins

Est. Total Time: 50 mins

Ingredients

- 1 ½ pounds 93%-lean ground turkey
- ½ cup panko breadcrumbs
- ¼ cup grated red onion, plus 3/4 cup quartered and thinly sliced
- 1 large egg, lightly beaten
- 1 tablespoon minced fresh oregano plus 2 tsp., or 1 1/2 tsp. dried oregano, divided
- 3 teaspoons minced garlic, divided
- 2 teaspoons olive oil plus 3 Tbsp., divided
- ¾ teaspoon salt

- ½ teaspoon ground pepper
- 3 (6 inch) whole-wheat pita breads
- 3 tablespoons red-wine vinegar
- 1 teaspoon honey
- 1 teaspoon Dijon mustard
- 1 large English cucumber, sliced
- 1 ¾ cups diced plum tomatoes (3-5 tomatoes)
- ¾ cup sliced pitted Kalamata olives

Instructions

- Set the oven to 425 degrees Fahrenheit. Spray cooking oil on a sizable baking sheet with a rim.
- In a sizable bowl, combine the turkey, breadcrumbs, grated onion, egg, 1 Tbsp. fresh oregano (or 1 tsp. dried), 2 Tbsp. garlic, 2 Tbsp. oil, salt, and pepper. Form the mixture into 42 meatballs, each measuring about 1 inch in diameter,

using a tablespoon. Place on the baking sheet that has been prepared. The meatballs should bake for 10 to 12 minutes, or until browned and an instant-read thermometer inserted in the center reads 165 degrees F.

- Pitas can be torn into half-moon shapes after being split in half horizontally into thin rounds.

- Place in the oven for 5 to 7 minutes, or until golden brown and crisp. Pitas should be broken into little croutons after cooling.

- In a large bowl, combine the vinegar, remaining 3 Tbsp. of oil, 2 tsp. of fresh oregano (or 1/2 tsp. dried), 1 tsp. of garlic, honey, and mustard. Toss together after adding the cucumber, tomatoes, olives, and onion slices. Add the pita croutons and stir. Along with the meatballs, serve the salad.

Coconut Curry Shrimp

Servings : 6

34.4 grams Protein

37.1 grams Carb

10.3 grams Fat

378 Cal Per Serving

Est. Active Time: 30 mins

Est. Total Time: 35 mins

Ingredients

- 2 tablespoons canola oil
- 3 tablespoons green curry paste
- 1 tablespoon finely chopped garlic
- 1 tablespoon finely chopped fresh ginger
- 1 ½ teaspoons finely chopped lemongrass
- 1 (15 ounce) can light coconut milk, well shaken
- 1 cup reduced-sodium vegetable broth
- 1 ½ teaspoons fish sauce
- 2 teaspoons cornstarch

- 6 ounces snow peas, cut into 1-inch pieces
- 1 cup matchstick-cut carrots
- 2 pounds medium shrimp, peeled and deveined
- ½ cup packed fresh Thai basil or Italian basil, thinly sliced
- 3 cups hot cooked brown rice

Instructions

- Oil is heated in a big pot over a medium heat. Add the curry paste, garlic, ginger, and lemongrass. Stir constantly for 2 minutes, or until the mixture is fragrant and dry. Stir to remove any browned bits from the pan's bottom before adding the coconut milk and broth. Heat to a rolling boil over medium-high. Reduce heat to medium-low; simmer 5 minutes undisturbed.

- In a small bowl, combine cornstarch and fish sauce. Stir into the curry mixture, then heat to a boil. Reduce the heat to medium-low; simmer for about 5 minutes, stirring periodically, until the sauce starts to thicken.
- Adding carrots and snow peas will cause the curry sauce to boil again over medium-high heat.
- Unflinchingly boil for 2 minutes or until the vegetables are soft. Add the shrimp; simmer for about 2 minutes, stirring periodically, or until the shrimp become pink and are cooked through. Stir in basil after removing from heat. Over rice, please.

Cilantro-Lime Chicken Tacos

Servings : 4

32 grams Protein

23 grams Carb

18 grams Fat

385 Cal Per Serving

Est. Active Time: 45 mins

Est. Total Time: 1hr 45 mins

Ingredients

- 1 cup loosely packed cilantro leaves, plus 1/4 cup chopped fresh cilantro, divided
- ¼ cup olive oil
- ½ teaspoon lime zest (reserve before juicing limes)
- 3 tablespoons lime juice, divided
- 2 tablespoons orange juice
- 2 cloves garlic, minced
- ¼ teaspoon salt plus 1/8 tsp., divided

- 1 ¼ pounds thin-sliced boneless, skinless chicken cutlets
- 1 cup diced tomatoes
- 1 cup diced strawberries
- 1 tablespoon minced jalapeño pepper
- 2 cups baby spinach
- 8 (6 inch) blue or yellow corn tortillas, warmed

Instructions

- 1 cup cilantro leaves, oil, 2 tablespoons each of lime and orange juice, garlic, and 1/4 teaspoon salt should all be combined in a food processor or blender and blend until smooth. Refrigerate half of the mixture after transferring it to a small bowl.
- Chicken should be added to the remaining ingredients in a sealable plastic bag. Coat the chicken with seal

and a turn. For 30 to 60 minutes, refrigerate.

- Meanwhile, in a medium bowl, combine tomatoes, strawberries, jalapenos, lime zest, remaining 1 Tbsp. lime juice, 1/4 cup chopped cilantro, and 1/8 tsp. salt; toss well. Keep chilled until you're ready to serve.

- Set the grill to medium-high heat. Grill grate should be lightly oiled. Chicken should be taken out of the marinade (discard the marinade).

- Grill the chicken for 4 to 5 minutes per side, or until it is thoroughly browned. (An other method is to broil the chicken for 4 to 5 minutes per side.) Give the chicken five minutes to rest. Cut into long, thin strips.

- To assemble, top each tortilla with a generous 1/3 cup of chicken and 1/4 cup spinach. Each should have 1/4 cup salsa and roughly 1 1/2 teaspoons of the remaining cilantro mixture on top.

Grilled Flank Steak with Tomato Salad

Servings : 4

25.3 grams Protein

3.9 grams Carb

25.1 grams Fat

346 Cal Per Serving

Est. Active Time: 10 mins

Est. Total Time: 20 mins

Ingredients

- 1 pint grape tomatoes, halved
- ½ cup chopped fresh cilantro
- ⅓ cup extra-virgin olive oil
- 1 small jalapeño pepper, seeded and sliced
- 2 teaspoons finely chopped garlic
- ½ teaspoon salt, divided
- 1 1-pound flank steak
- ½ teaspoon ground pepper

Instructions

- Set the grill to medium-high heat or preheat the grill pan.
- In a medium bowl, mix the tomatoes, cilantro, oil, jalapenos, garlic, and 1/4 teaspoon salt.
- Add the final 1/4 teaspoon of salt and pepper to the meat. Grill for 3 to 5 minutes on each side or until an instant-read thermometer inserted in the center registers 125 degrees F for medium-rare.
- Slice the steak thinly across the grain on a clean cutting board, preferably one with grooves for catching juices. Four platters should receive the slices. Top the steak with the tomato salad and any liquids that have gathered on the cutting board.

Chicken & Zucchini Casserole

Servings : 8

33.6 grams Protein

11.1 grams Carb

13.8 grams Fat

307 Cal Per Serving

Est. Active Time: 30 mins

Est. Total Time: 95 mins

Ingredients

- 3 tablespoons butter, divided
- 2 pounds boneless, skinless chicken breast, cut into 1-inch pieces
- 2 large zucchini, cut into 1/2-inch pieces
- 1 large red bell pepper, chopped
- ⅓ cup all-purpose flour
- 1 cup no-salt-added chicken broth
- 1 cup whole milk
- 3 ounces reduced-fat cream cheese

- 1 ¼ cups shredded part-skim mozzarella cheese, divided
- ¾ teaspoon ground pepper
- ½ teaspoon salt

Instructions

- Set the oven to 400 degrees Fahrenheit. Using a large skillet over medium-high heat, melt 1 tablespoon of butter. Add the chicken to the pan and cook it for about 8 minutes, stirring regularly, until it is thoroughly browned. Take the chicken and place it in a medium bowl. Add the bell pepper and zucchini to the pan; simmer, stirring occasionally, for 4 minutes, or until the vegetables begin to soften. Place the chicken and the zucchini mixture in a bowl.
- The pan will now need the final 2 tablespoons of butter. Add the flour and

stir continuously while cooking for about a minute, or until the flour begins to brown. Add the milk and broth and stir frequently as it boils. Remove from heat and mix in 3/4 cup mozzarella and cream cheese until melted. Add salt and pepper and stir.

- Stir the chicken and veggies into the cheese sauce after draining the liquid from the chicken and vegetable mixture. Place in a 2-quart baking pan. Spread the remaining 1/2 cup of cheese over the casserole and place it on a baking sheet lined with foil.
- Bake for 20 to 25 minutes, or until the top is browned and the edges are bubbling. Let stand for 10 minutes before serving.

Egg Roll-Inspired Cabbage Rolls

Servings : 6

20.4 grams Protein

28.2 grams Carb

4.8 grams Fat

231 Cal Per Serving

Est. Active Time: 45 mins

Est. Total Time: 90 mins

Ingredients

- 1 ¼ cups water
- 3 tablespoons tomato paste
- 2 tablespoons rice vinegar
- 2 tablespoons reduced-sodium soy sauce
- 4 tablespoons hoisin sauce, divided
- 2 tablespoons minced fresh ginger, divided
- 4 cloves garlic, minced, divided
- ½ teaspoon crushed red pepper
- 2 tablespoons cornstarch

- 12 large leaves savoy cabbage
- 2 cups finely chopped broccoli
- 1 pound lean ground pork
- 1 ½ cups cooked brown rice
- 1 bunch scallions, sliced
- 1 teaspoon toasted sesame oil

Instructions

- Set the oven to 400 °F. Spray cooking oil in a 9 by 13-inch baking pan.
- In a small saucepan, combine the following ingredients: water, tomato paste, vinegar, soy sauce, 2 teaspoons hoisin, 1 tablespoon ginger, 2 cloves garlic, and crushed red pepper. Add cornstarch and boil while stirring over medium-high heat. Cook for about 2 minutes while stirring to thicken. Heat has been removed; set aside.

- In the meantime, heat up a sizable pot of water to a boil. Four cabbage leaves should be added and cooked for one to two minutes while gently stirring. Transfer to a baking sheet with a rim. Use the remaining cabbage leaves to repeat the process. Put the broccoli in a colander and cover it with hot water. Use cold water to rehydrate. Place in a large bowl.

- Include the remaining 2 teaspoons of hoisin, 1 tablespoon of ginger, 2 cloves of garlic, 3 tablespoons of the sauce that was set aside, rice, scallions, sesame oil, and the pork. Mix thoroughly by stirring.

- Over the bottom part of 1 softened cabbage leaf, spread 1/3 cup of the filling. Roll up after folding the bottom and sides over the filling. Put in the baking dish that has been prepared, seam-side down. Repeat with the rest of the filling and leaves. Over the rolls, spread the remaining sauce. When an instant-read thermometer inserted into the center of a roll reads 150°F, cover with foil and bake for 40 minutes.

Easy Shrimp Tacos

Servings : 4

29 grams Protein

34 grams Carb

16 grams Fat

398 Cal Per Serving

Est. Active Time: 30 mins

Est. Total Time: 30 mins

Ingredients

- 2 cups diced tomatoes
- 1 teaspoon lime zest
- 5 tablespoons lime juice, divided
- ¼ cup chopped fresh cilantro
- ¼ cup diced red onion
- 2 tablespoons minced jalapeño pepper
- ⅛ teaspoon salt
- 2 tablespoons tahini
- ½ teaspoon honey
- 1 clove garlic, minced

- 2 tablespoons olive oil
- 1 tablespoon ground cumin
- 2 teaspoons ground coriander
- ¼ teaspoon ground pepper
- 1 pound large raw shrimp peeled and deveined
- 8 (6 inch) flour tortillas, warmed
- 1 cup thinly sliced radishes

Instructions

- Heat the broiler. In a medium bowl, add tomatoes, 2 tablespoons lime juice, cilantro, onion, jalapeno, and salt; toss to blend.
- In a small bowl, combine the lime zest, remaining 3 tbsp. of lime juice, tahini, honey, and garlic.
- In a big bowl, mix the pepper, oil, cumin, and coriander. Add the shrimp and coat well. On a sizable baking sheet with a

rim, spread out the shrimp. For 4 to 6 minutes, broil the shrimp, tossing once, until they are pink and barely cooked through.

- Put 2 to 3 shrimp on each tortilla to construct. About 3 Tbsp. salsa, 2 tsp. tahini sauce, and 2 Tbsp. radishes should be added to each.

Quinoa-Stuffed Peppers

Servings : 4

15.7 grams Protein

43.9 grams Carb

12.8 grams Fat

350 Cal Per Serving

Est. Active Time: 25 mins

Est. Total Time: 45 mins

Ingredients

- 6 medium red, orange and/or yellow bell peppers
- 1 tablespoon extra-virgin olive oil
- 1 large yellow onion, chopped (about 2 cups)
- 1 tablespoon minced garlic
- 1 teaspoon ground cumin
- ¾ teaspoon chili powder
- 2 teaspoons minced chipotle chiles plus 1 Tbsp. adobo sauce from can

- 2 cups cooked tri-color quinoa
- 1 (15 ounce) can no-salt-added black beans, rinsed
- 1 (14.5 ounce) can no-salt-added diced tomatoes
- 1 cup frozen corn
- ¼ teaspoon salt
- 1 ½ cups shredded pepper Jack cheese

Instructions

- Set the oven to 375 degrees Fahrenheit. Each bell pepper should have its stem removed. To make 1 cup, finely chop the pepper tops. Pepper seeds and membranes should be removed and discarded. In a big pot with a steamer basket, bring about one inch of water to a boil. Add the peppers; cover and steam for 3 minutes, or until they begin to soften. Peppers removed, placed aside.

- A big skillet with medium heat is used to heat the oil. Cook, stirring occasionally, until the onion is transparent, about 5 minutes after adding the onion and the chopped pepper tops. Add the garlic, cumin, chili powder, chipotles, and adobo; stir frequently for about a minute, until aromatic.
- Remove from the heat and stir in the quinoa, black beans, tomatoes, corn, and salt.
- Place the peppers in an 11 by 7-inch baking dish standing up. (If necessary, trim the bottoms to keep the peppers standing.) Fill each pepper securely with the quinoa mixture by spooning roughly 1 cup into each one. Wrap foil around the stuffed peppers.
- Bake the peppers for 10 minutes or until well heated. After removing the foil,

evenly distribute the cheese over the peppers. Bake uncovered for 5 to 8 minutes, or until the cheese melts and starts to color. Before serving, allow it to rest for five minutes.

Instant-Pot Sausage & Peppers

Servings : 4

25.2 grams Protein

38.9 grams Carb

12.6 grams Fat

374 Cal Per Serving

Est. Active Time: 25 mins

Est. Total Time: 45 mins

Ingredients

- 1 tablespoon extra-virgin olive oil
- 1 (12 ounce) package hot or mild Italian chicken sausage
- 1 large white onion, sliced
- 1 medium yellow bell pepper, sliced
- 1 medium green bell pepper, sliced
- 1 large garlic clove, minced
- ½ teaspoon dried oregano
- ¼ teaspoon crushed red pepper
- 1 tablespoon no-salt-added tomato paste

- ½ (15 ounce) can no-salt-added crushed tomatoes
- 4 Italian sandwich rolls, split and lightly toasted
- ¼ cup torn fresh basil

Instructions

- On a programmable pressure multicooker, choose the Sauté setting (such as Instant Pot; times, instructions and settings may vary according to cooker brand or model). Choose the Medium setting and heat for 1–2 minutes. Cooker with oil and sausage added.
- Cook for 4 to 5 minutes on each side, rotating halfway through, until browned. Take out of the cooker, then place aside. Don't clean the burner with a cloth.

- Add the onion, yellow pepper, and green pepper while the heat is still on medium. Cook, stirring occasionally, for about 5 minutes, or until the vegetables are soft and beginning to brown. Add garlic, oregano and crushed red pepper; cook, stirring occasionally, until fragrant, about 2 minutes.
- Cook the tomato paste for 1 minute, scraping the bottom of the pan to loosen any browned bits and stirring continuously. Return the sausages to the stove after stirring in the smashed tomatoes. Select Cancel.
- Put the lid on the cooker and secure it. Set the sealing position on the steam release handle. Decide on Manual/Pressure Cook. For 5 minutes, choose High pressure. (The cooker will

need 12 to 15 minutes to reach pressure before cooking can start.

- Turn the steam release handle slowly to the Venting position once the cooking is complete in order to allow the steam to completely escape. The cooker's lid should be removed.

- Divide the sausage, onions, and peppers among the rolls using a slotted spoon. Add basil on top. Serve right away.

Chicken Cutlets with Creamy Spinach & Roasted Red Pepper Sauce

Servings : 4

28.2 grams Protein

10.3 grams Carb

13.5 grams Fat

305 Cal Per Serving

Est. Active Time: 20 mins

Est. Total Time: 20 mins

Ingredients

- 1 pound chicken cutlets
- ¼ teaspoon salt, divided
- ¼ teaspoon ground pepper, divided
- 1 tablespoon extra-virgin olive oil
- 1 cup chopped baby spinach
- ½ cup finely chopped red onion
- ⅓ cup roasted red peppers, thinly sliced
- ⅓ cup sun-dried tomato halves, thinly sliced
- ½ cup dry white wine

- ¾ cup sour cream

Instructions

- Add salt and pepper to chicken with a 1/8 teaspoon each. In a sizable skillet, heat the oil over medium-high heat. Add the chicken and heat for 6 to 8 minutes, flipping once, or until thoroughly done. Place on a platter.
- Sun-dried tomatoes, spinach, onion, and roasted red peppers should all be added to the pan. Cook for one minute while stirring. Add wine and turn the heat up to high.
- Cook for approximately two minutes, scraping off any browned parts as you go, or until the liquid has mostly evaporated. Stir in sour cream, any leftover chicken juices, and the final 1/8 teaspoon of salt and pepper.

- Lower heat to medium and simmer for 2 minutes while stirring. Turn the chicken back in the pan to coat it. Serve the sauced chicken on a plate.

Spicy Noodles with Pork, Scallions & Bok Choy

Servings :6

20.1 grams Protein

38.6 grams Carb

9.1 grams Fat

311 Cal Per Serving

Est. Active Time: 35 mins

Est. Total Time: 35 mins

Ingredients

- 7 ounces thin rice noodles or rice sticks
- 2 tablespoons canola oil, divided
- 1 head bok choy (about 1 pound), chopped, greens and whites separated
- 3 scallions, sliced, greens and whites separated
- 2 tablespoons minced fresh ginger
- ¼ cup chili-bean sauce or chile-garlic sauce
- 1 pound ground pork

- 2 cups unsalted chicken broth
- 3 tablespoons reduced-sodium tamari or soy sauce
- 1 teaspoon white sugar
- 1 tablespoon cornstarch
- 1 tablespoon water
- Crushed red pepper for garnish

Instructions

- Noodles should be prepared as directed on the packaging. Drain and then run a cold water rinse. Place aside
- In the meantime, heat 1 tablespoon of oil in a sizable cast-iron pan or wok with a flat bottom over high heat. Bok choy whites are added and cooked for 1 minute while stirring. Bok choy greens should be added and cooked for an additional minute or so, or until wilted. Place all of the bok choy in a bowl.

- Scallion whites, ginger, chili-bean sauce (or chili-garlic sauce), and the final tablespoon of oil should all be added to the pan. With a wooden spoon, crumble the pork as it cooks for 3 to 5 minutes, or until it is no longer pink. Tie together sugar, tamari (or soy sauce), and broth. In a small bowl, combine the cornstarch and water; add to the pan.
- Bring to a boil and simmer while stirring for one minute or until slightly thickened. Add the saved noodles and bok choy, and stir-fry for about a minute, or until heated through. If preferred, garnish with crushed red pepper and scallion greens before serving.

Shrimp Cauliflower Fried Rice

Servings :4

30.1 grams Protein

9.6 grams Carb

16.9 grams Fat

309 Cal Per Serving

Est. Active Time: 25 mins

Est. Total Time: 25 mins

Ingredients

- ¼ cup sesame oil, divided
- 2 large eggs, lightly beaten
- 3 cups riced cauliflower
- 1 pound large shrimp (31-35 count), peeled and deveined
- 3 cups broccoli florets
- 1 medium red bell pepper, thinly sliced (about 1 cup)
- 3 cloves garlic, sliced

- 3 tablespoons reduced-sodium soy sauce or tamari
- 2 tablespoons water
- 1 tablespoon rice vinegar
- ½ teaspoon ground pepper

Instructions

- In a large, heavy skillet or wok with a flat bottom made of carbon steel, heat 2 tablespoons of oil over high heat. Add the eggs and fry them for about 30 seconds, flipping them only once, without stirring. About 15 seconds after flipping, fry the other side until just done. Cut into 1/2-inch pieces after transferring to a cutting board.
- Heat the pan on a high heat while adding 2 teaspoons of oil. Cauliflower should be added in an equal layer; cook 3 to 4

minutes, stirring occasionally, until gently browned. Place on a platter.

- Heat the pan on a high heat while adding 2 teaspoons of oil. Add the shrimp; cook, tossing frequently, for about 3 minutes, or until just opaque. Place on the same platter as the cauliflower.

- Over high heat, add the remaining 2 tablespoons of oil to the pan.

- Add the broccoli, bell pepper, and garlic; simmer for 4 to 5 minutes, stirring periodically, until the broccoli is gently browned. Add pepper, vinegar, water, soy sauce (or tamari), and to taste. Boil for 30 seconds after bringing to a boil. Get rid of the heat. Add the shrimp, cauliflower, and saved eggs to the mixture.

Shepherd's Pie with Cauliflower Topping

Servings :6

20 grams Protein

18.1 grams Carb

23.2 grams Fat

356 Cal Per Serving

Est. Active Time: 35 mins

Est. Total Time: 60 mins

Ingredients

- 1 pound lean ground beef
- 2 cups chopped onion
- 2 tablespoons minced garlic
- 1 (15 ounce) can no-salt-added diced tomatoes, drained
- 1 tablespoon reduced-sodium Worcestershire sauce
- 1 ½ teaspoons chopped fresh rosemary
- 3 tablespoons chopped fresh flat-leaf parsley, divided

- 1 ½ teaspoons ground pepper, divided
- ¾ teaspoon salt, divided
- ¼ cup unsalted beef broth
- 1 tablespoon all-purpose flour or gluten-free all-purpose flour
- 8 cups cauliflower florets (from 1 large head cauliflower)
- 2 cups water
- 6 tablespoons unsalted butter
- ¼ cup heavy cream

Instructions

- Set the oven to 375 degrees Fahrenheit. A 12-inch oven-safe skillet is heated to medium-high heat. Add the beef, onion, and garlic; simmer for 8 to 10 minutes, stirring frequently to break up the steak. Add the Worcestershire sauce, rosemary, 1 tablespoon parsley, 1 teaspoon pepper, and 1/4 teaspoon salt after you've added the drained tomatoes.

- In a small bowl, combine the flour and broth; then toss the mixture in the skillet. Cook the mixture for about 15 minutes, stirring often over medium-low heat.

- Cauliflower and water should be combined in a big pot and heated to a boil. For about 10 minutes, or until the cauliflower is soft when poked with a fork, simmer with the lid on over medium-high heat. Drain.

- Add the remaining 1/2 teaspoon of salt, the butter, and the cream. Mash with a fork or a potato masher until smooth (you will have about 4 cups mashed).

- Spread the mashed cauliflower evenly over the heated mixture in the skillet using a careful spoon (do not mix the 2 layers together). Add the final 1/2 teaspoon of pepper on top.

- Bake for 22 to 25 minutes, or until the filling is bubbling and the top is starting to brown. Before serving, top with the final 2 tablespoons of parsley.

Creamy Lemon Pasta with Shrimp

Servings :4

28.3 grams Protein

18.1 grams Carb

13.9 grams Fat

403 Cal Per Serving

Est. Active Time: 20 mins

Est. Total Time: 20 mins

Ingredients

- 8 ounces whole-wheat fettuccine
- 1 tablespoon extra-virgin olive oil
- 12 ounces peeled and deveined raw shrimp (21-25 count)
- 2 tablespoons unsalted butter
- 1 tablespoon finely chopped garlic
- ¼ teaspoon crushed red pepper
- 4 cups loosely packed arugula
- ¼ cup whole-milk plain yogurt
- 1 teaspoon lemon zest

- 2 tablespoons lemon juice
- ¼ teaspoon salt
- ⅓ cup grated Parmesan cheese, plus more for garnish
- ¼ cup thinly sliced fresh basil

Instructions

- 7 cups of water should come to a boil. Stir the fettuccine to separate the noodles before adding. Cook for 7 to 9 minutes, or until the meat is barely tender. After draining, save 1/2 cup of the cooking liquid.
- Over medium-high heat, warm oil in a sizable nonstick skillet. Add the shrimp and cook, stirring periodically, for 2 to 3 minutes, or until pink and curled. Put the shrimp in a basin.
- Reduce heat to medium, then add butter to the pan. Stir often while cooking the

garlic and crushed red pepper for approximately a minute, or until the garlic is aromatic. Arugula should be added and cooked for about a minute while stirring. Low-heat setting.

- When the pasta is thoroughly coated and creamy, add the remaining 1/4 cup of cooking water, the yogurt, the lemon zest, and the fettuccine. Add the salt, lemon juice, and shrimp while tossing the fettuccine to coat. Take the dish off the heat, then top with Parmesan.

- If preferred, top the fettuccine with additional Parmesan and basil.

Spinach Ravioli with Artichokes & Olives

Servings :4

15 grams Protein

60.9 grams Carb

19.2 grams Fat

454 Cal Per Serving

Est. Active Time: 15 mins

Est. Total Time: 15 mins

Ingredients

- 2 (8 ounce) packages frozen or refrigerated spinach-and-ricotta ravioli
- ½ cup oil-packed sun-dried tomatoes, drained (2 tablespoons oil reserved)
- 1 (10 ounce) package frozen quartered artichoke hearts, thawed
- 1 (15 ounce) can no-salt-added cannellini beans, rinsed
- ¼ cup Kalamata olives, sliced
- 3 tablespoons toasted pine nuts
- ¼ cup chopped fresh basil

Instructions

- Bring water in a big pot to a boil. Cook ravioli as directed on the package. Drain, then toss with 1 tablespoon of the saved oil.
- In a big nonstick skillet, heat the last tablespoon of oil over medium heat. Add the beans and artichokes, and cook for 2 to 3 minutes, or until cooked through.
- Add basil, sun-dried tomatoes, olives, cooked ravioli, and pine nuts after folding.

Lemon-Garlic Chicken with Green Beans

Servings :4

26.5 grams Protein

11.1 grams Carb

15.7 grams Fat

296 Cal Per Serving

Est. Active Time: 20 mins

Est. Total Time: 20 mins

Ingredients

- 1 pound chicken breast cutlets
- 1 teaspoon salt, divided
- ½ teaspoon ground pepper, divided
- 2 tablespoons extra-virgin olive oil, divided
- 6 cups green beans (about 1 pound), trimmed
- 4 cloves garlic, thinly sliced
- 1 teaspoon grated lemon zest

- 1 teaspoon chopped fresh thyme, plus leaves for garnish
- ¼ cup unsalted chicken broth
- ¼ cup dry white wine
- 1 tablespoon lemon juice
- ¼ cup toasted pine nuts
- Lemon wedges for garnish

Instructions

- 1/4 teaspoon pepper and 1/2 teaspoon salt should be added to the chicken. In a large skillet over medium-high heat, warm 1 tablespoon of oil. Cook the chicken for 3 to 4 minutes on each side, turning it once, or until an instant-read thermometer inserted in the thickest section reads 165 degrees F. Place on a platter.
- Green beans and the final tablespoon of oil are added to the pan. Add the

remaining 1/2 teaspoon salt and 1/4 teaspoon pepper, then sauté for approximately 2 minutes, stirring periodically, until tender-crisp. Add the garlic, lemon zest, and thyme, and stir-fry for about a minute, until aromatic. Return the chicken to the pan along with any accumulated juices, then add the broth, wine, and lemon juice.

- Cook for another minute or so, stirring regularly, until the liquid has been cut in half.
- If preferred, garnish with pine nuts, more thyme, and lemon wedges before serving.

Polenta Bowls with Roasted Vegetables & Fried Eggs

Servings :4

20 grams Protein

44.2 grams Carb

22.2 grams Fat

453 Cal Per Serving

Est. Active Time: 30 mins

Est. Total Time: 30 mins

Ingredients

- 6 large shallots, halved lengthwise
- 3 tablespoons olive oil, divided
- 1 pound thick asparagus spears, trimmed and cut into 2-inch pieces
- 6 ounces cremini mushrooms, halved lengthwise
- 3 tablespoons balsamic vinegar
- 1 tablespoon chopped fresh thyme
- ½ teaspoon ground pepper
- ½ teaspoon salt, divided

- 2 cups whole milk
- 2 cups unsalted chicken stock
- ¾ cup instant polenta
- ½ cup grated Parmesan cheese
- 4 large eggs

Instructions

- Set the oven to 425 degrees Fahrenheit. Wrap foil around a sizable baking sheet with a rim. Toss the shallots in 1 tablespoon oil after placing them on the preheated pan. 12 minutes of roasting time or until lightly browned.
- In the pan with the shallots, add the asparagus, mushrooms, vinegar, thyme, pepper, 1/4 teaspoon salt, and 1 tablespoon oil. To coat, stir. For about 8 minutes, roast the vegetables until they are just tender.

- In the meantime, put the milk and stock in a big pot and heat it up to a boil. Add polenta and stir. Lower heat to medium-low; cook for 4 to 5 minutes, stirring frequently, until thickened. Stir in Parmesan after removing from heat.
- A sizable nonstick skillet with the remaining 1 tablespoon oil should be heated over medium-high heat.
- One at a time, add eggs; using a rubber spatula to keep the eggs apart, cook for 2 to 3 minutes, or until the whites are fully cooked but the yolks are still slightly runny.
- Place a generous amount of polenta into four small bowls. Add vegetables and eggs, and then top with the remaining 1/4 teaspoon salt.

Salt & Vinegar Sheet-Pan Chicken & Brussels Sprouts

Servings : 4

35.5 grams Protein

19.9 grams Carb

18.8 grams Fat

387 Cal Per Serving

Est. Active Time: 20 mins

Est. Total Time: 45 mins

Ingredients

- 1 ½ pounds bone-in, skin-on chicken breasts
- 3 tablespoons extra-virgin olive oil, divided
- 1 teaspoon kosher salt, divided
- ½ teaspoon ground pepper, divided
- 1 ½ pounds Brussels sprouts, trimmed and halved or quartered if large
- 2 medium red onions, cut into 1/2-inch wedges

- 6 tablespoons malt vinegar or sherry vinegar
- ½ teaspoon dried dill
- ½ teaspoon garlic powder
- ½ teaspoon onion powder
- ¼ teaspoon sugar

Instructions

- Set oven to 450 degrees Fahrenheit.
- Divide a chicken breast into four equal pieces. 1 tablespoon of oil should be used to brush, and 1/4 teaspoon of salt and pepper should be added. The remaining 2 tablespoons of oil, together with 1/4 teaspoons of salt and pepper, are added to the large bowl of Brussels sprouts and onions. On a baking sheet with a rim, arrange the chicken, veggies, and mushrooms in a single layer.

- Roast for 20 to 25 minutes, or until the veggies are soft and an instant-read thermometer put into the thickest part of a breast without touching the bone reads 160 degrees F.
- In the meantime, combine vinegar, sugar, dill, onion, garlic, and garlic powder in a tiny microwave-safe bowl. About 30 seconds on High in the microwave will get the salt and sugar to dissolve.
- Add the vinegar mixture to the chicken and vegetables, then roast for a further five minutes. While stirring the veggies in the skillet, remove the chicken to a serving plate. Along with the chicken, serve the vegetables.

Spicy Noodles with Pork, Scallions & Bok Choy

Servings : 6

20.1 grams Protein

38.6 grams Carb

9.1 grams Fat

311 Cal Per Serving

Est. Active Time: 35 mins

Est. Total Time: 35 mins

Ingredients

- 7 ounces thin rice noodles or rice sticks
- 2 tablespoons canola oil, divided
- 1 head bok choy (about 1 pound), chopped, greens and whites separated
- 3 scallions, sliced, greens and whites separated
- 2 tablespoons minced fresh ginger
- ¼ cup chili-bean sauce or chile-garlic sauce
- 1 pound ground pork

- 2 cups unsalted chicken broth
- 3 tablespoons reduced-sodium tamari or soy sauce
- 1 teaspoon white sugar
- 1 tablespoon cornstarch
- 1 tablespoon water
- Crushed red pepper for garnish

Instructions

- Noodles should be prepared as directed on the packaging. Drain and then run a cold water rinse. Place aside.
- In the meantime, heat 1 tablespoon of oil in a sizable cast-iron pan or wok with a flat bottom over high heat. Bok choy whites are added and cooked for 1 minute while stirring. Bok choy greens should be added and cooked for an additional minute or so, or until wilted. Place all of the bok choy in a bowl.

- Scallion whites, ginger, chili-bean sauce (or chili-garlic sauce), and the final tablespoon of oil should all be added to the pan. With a wooden spoon, crumble the pork as it cooks for 3 to 5 minutes, or until it is no longer pink. Tie together sugar, tamari (or soy sauce), and broth. In a small bowl, combine the cornstarch and water; add to the pan.

- Bring to a boil and simmer while stirring for one minute or until slightly thickened. Add the saved noodles and bok choy, and stir-fry for about a minute, or until heated through. If preferred, garnish with crushed red pepper and scallion greens before serving.

Honey-Garlic Chicken Thighs with Carrots & Broccoli

Servings : 4

35.8 grams Protein

39.7 grams Carb

20.1 grams Fat

475 Cal Per Serving

Est. Active Time: 20 mins

Est. Total Time: 75 mins

Ingredients

- ⅓ cup honey
- 1 ½ tablespoons reduced sodium soy sauce or tamari
- 4 cloves garlic, minced (about 1 1/2 tablespoons)
- 1 tablespoon cider vinegar
- ¼ teaspoon crushed red pepper
- 8 (5 ounce) bone-in, skin-on chicken thighs

- 1 pound small carrots, sliced into 1/2-inch pieces
- 2 tablespoons olive oil, divided
- 4 cups broccoli florets (about 1 pound)
- ½ teaspoon salt
- ½ teaspoon ground pepper
- 1 teaspoon cornstarch
- 1 teaspoon water

Instructions

- In a small bowl, combine the honey, soy sauce (or tamari), garlic, vinegar, and red pepper flakes. In a zip-top plastic bag, combine chicken with 1/4 cup of the honey mixture; press out excess air; and close the bag. In the tightly closed bag, rub the chicken to thoroughly coat it. Refrigerate for up to two hours, but no more than 30 minutes. Keep the leftover honey mixture aside.

- Set the oven to 400 degrees Fahrenheit. Cooking spray should be used to cover the foil on a big baking sheet with a rim. Chicken should be taken out of the marinade and placed on one side of the prepared pan.

- In a medium bowl, add the carrots and 1 tablespoon of oil; toss to coat. On the opposite side of the pan, arrange the carrots in a uniform layer. For 15 minutes, bake the chicken and carrots. Stir the carrots after removing from the oven.

- Toss the broccoli thoroughly with the remaining 1 tbsp oil. Place the broccoli over the chicken and carrots in the pan in an equal layer. Season everything with salt & pepper. Bake for 15 to 18 minutes, or until a thermometer inserted in the thickest part of the chicken reads 165 degrees F and the vegetables are cooked.

- In the meantime, combine cornstarch and water in a small basin and stir until completely smooth.

- In a small saucepan, combine the cornstarch mixture with the honey mixture that was set aside; heat to a simmer while stirring once or twice. Stirring often, simmer for about 2 minutes or until the sauce is clear and thick. Over the chicken and vegetables, drizzle. Serve warm.

Easy Spicy Salmon Cakes

Servings : 4

16.4 grams Protein

20.1 grams Carb

19.8 grams Fat

330 Cal Per Serving

Est. Active Time: 20 mins

Est. Total Time: 20 mins

Ingredients

- 1 1/2 cups flaked cooked salmon
- 2 eggs, lightly beaten
- ¼ cup finely chopped red onion
- ¼ cup chopped fresh cilantro
- 1 tablespoon chile-garlic sauce
- 1 tablespoon low-sodium soy sauce
- 1 teaspoon Chinese five-spice powder
- 1 cup panko breadcrumbs
- ¼ cup canola oil

Instructions

- In a sizable bowl, mix the salmon, eggs, onion, cilantro, chile-garlic sauce, soy sauce, and five-spice powder. Stir in the breadcrumbs. Four 3-inch-wide patties should be formed.
- In a medium nonstick skillet, heat the oil over medium-high heat. Add the salmon cakes, and cook them for 4 to 6 minutes, turning them over after they are browned on both sides.

Chicken Parmesan & Quinoa Stuffed Peppers

Servings : 4

47.7 grams Protein

49.4 grams Carb

18.4 grams Fat

559 Cal Per Serving

Est. Active Time: 15 mins

Est. Total Time: 60 mins

Ingredients

- 1 tablespoon olive oil
- 1 medium onion, chopped (about 1 1/2 cups)
- 4 cloves garlic, minced
- 1 cup quinoa, rinsed
- 1 ¼ cups water
- 3 cups shredded cooked chicken breast
- 1 ½ cups lower-sodium marinara sauce
- ⅓ cup grated Parmesan cheese
- ¾ cup sliced fresh basil, divided

- 4 large red bell peppers (about 8 ounces each)
- 2 ounces low-moisture, part-skim mozzarella cheese, shredded (about 1/2 cup)

Instructions

- Set oven to 350 degrees Fahrenheit. Over medium-high heat, warm the oil in a medium saucepan. Add the onion and garlic; simmer, stirring occasionally, for 4 to 5 minutes, or until the onion is transparent. Add the quinoa and simmer for 30 seconds while stirring occasionally. Add water and bring to a boil on a high heat setting. Cook for 15 minutes with the heat reduced to medium. Remove from heat; cover and allow stand for five minutes. Chicken, marinara, Parmesan, and 1/2 cup basil are all stirred in.

- Remove seeds and membranes from peppers by trimming the top 1/2 inch. Place the peppers in an 8-inch-square glass baking dish with the sliced sides facing up. Microwave for three minutes on High while covering with plastic wrap. Unwrap the plastic.

- Distribute the quinoa mixture (approximately 1 1/4 cups per pepper half) equally within the pepper halves.

- For about 15 minutes, bake the filled peppers until they are tender. Sprinkle mozzarella evenly. Bake for another 5 to 7 minutes, or until the cheese has melted. Add the remaining 1/4 cup of basil evenly.

Scallion-Ginger Beef & Broccoli

Servings : 4

30 grams Protein

43.2 grams Carb

16 grams Fat

441 Cal Per Serving

Est. Active Time: 30 mins

Est. Total Time: 30 mins

Ingredients

- ⅓ cup reduced-sodium tamari or soy sauce
- ¼ cup low-sodium chicken broth
- 2 tablespoons brown sugar
- 2 tablespoons cornstarch, divided
- 1 pound sirloin steak, thinly sliced
- 3 tablespoons peanut or canola oil, divided
- 6 cups broccoli florets

- ½ cup sliced scallions, plus more for garnish
- 1 tablespoon finely grated ginger
- 1 teaspoon finely grated garlic
- 2 cups cooked brown rice
- Crushed red pepper for garnish

Instructions

- Brown sugar, broth, tamari (or soy sauce), and 1 tablespoon cornstarch are combined in a small bowl. Combine the remaining 1 tablespoon cornstarch with the steak.
- In a sizable cast-iron skillet or wok with a flat bottom, heat 2 tablespoons of oil over high heat. Add the steak and simmer for 4 minutes, stirring once, or until browned. Place on a fresh dish. Broccoli and the remaining 1 tablespoon of oil should be added.

- Cook for 2 minutes, stirring occasionally. Add the scallions, ginger, and garlic, and stir-fry for about 30 seconds, or until fragrant. Return the meat to the pan and stir the tamari mixture; simmer for one minute or until the sauce thickens. Serve with red pepper flakes on top of the brown rice, if preferred.

Baked Halibut with Brussels Sprouts & Quinoa

Servings : 4

29.7 grams Protein

36.1 grams Carb

17.1 grams Fat

406 Cal Per Serving

Est. Active Time: 15 mins

Est. Total Time: 30 mins

Ingredients

- 1 pound Brussels sprouts, trimmed and sliced
- 1 fennel bulb, trimmed and cut into strips
- 1 tablespoon plus 1 teaspoon olive oil, divided
- ½ teaspoon salt, divided
- ½ teaspoon ground pepper, divided
- 1 (1 pound) halibut filet, cut into 4 portions
- 4 cloves garlic, minced, divided

- 3 tablespoons lemon juice
- 2 tablespoons unsalted butter, melted
- 2 cups cooked quinoa
- ¼ cup chopped sun-dried tomatoes
- ¼ cup chopped pitted Kalamata olives
- 2 tablespoons chopped fresh Italian parsley or fennel fronds

Instructions

- Oven rack placement and temperature adjustment to 400 degrees Fahrenheit.
- In a sizable bowl, combine the Brussels sprouts, fennel, 1 Tbsp. of oil, and 1/4 tsp. of salt and pepper; toss to coat. On a sizable baking sheet with a rim, spread out in a single layer. Bake for 20 to 25 minutes, stirring periodically, until soft.
- Halibut should now be placed on a different sizable rimmed baking sheet, along with half of the garlic and the final

1/4 tsp. of salt and pepper. In a small bowl, mix the melted butter and lemon juice. Half of the mixture should be drizzled or brushed on the fish. Bake for 12 to 15 minutes, or until the salmon is opaque and flakes readily with a fork.

- Quinoa, the remaining 1 tsp. oil, sun-dried tomatoes, olives, and parsley (or fennel fronds) should all be combined in a medium bowl at this time.

- To the lemon-butter mixture, incorporate the remaining garlic. After pouring the mixture over the vegetables, bake for an additional minute. Serve the quinoa mixture with the halibut and vegetables.

Stuffed Sweet Potatoes with Chili

Servings : 4

20.1 grams Protein

26.8 grams Carb

9.1 grams Fat

266 Cal Per Serving

Est. Active Time: 20 mins

Est. Total Time: 70 mins

Ingredients

- 2 small sweet potatoes (about 8 oz. each)
- 1 tablespoon canola oil
- 8 ounces 95%-lean ground beef
- 2 scallions, sliced, green and white parts separated
- 2 tablespoons tomato paste
- 1-2 canned chipotle peppers in adobo, chopped
- 1 tablespoon paprika
- ¼ teaspoon salt

- 1 cup canned low-sodium kidney beans, rinsed
- ½ cup water
- ¼ cup shredded Mexican-blend cheese
- 4 teaspoons reduced-fat sour cream for garnish

Instructions

- Set the oven to 425 degrees Fahrenheit. A baking sheet should be foil-lined.
- Place the sweet potatoes on the preheated pan after giving them many fork pricks. Bake for 40 to 45 minutes, or until a knife inserted comes out clean. Allow to cool a bit.
- Oil should be heated in a big skillet while doing this. Add ground beef and the whites of the scallions. Cook the beef, tossing and breaking it up with a wooden spoon, for about 4 minutes, or until it is

no longer pink. Add salt, paprika, chipotles, and tomato paste as desired. About 1 minute, while stirring, cook the tomato paste until it starts to brown. Cook, stirring, the water and beans mixture for another minute or more, or until the majority of the liquid has evaporated. Cover up to stay warm.

- The sweet potatoes should be cut in half lengthwise. Scoop the flesh into a medium bowl while preserving the skins. Stir in 1 cup of the chili mixture after adding it. Place the sweet potato-chili mixture inside each potato skin (the skins will be full). Re-add the cheese and remaining chili mixture to the baking sheet.

- Bake for 3 to 5 minutes, or until the cheese is melted and the potatoes are well heated. If desired, add sour cream as a garnish and top with scallion greens.

Piled-High Vegetable Pitas

Servings : 4

15.1 grams Protein

52.7 grams Carb

14.8 grams Fat

399 Cal Per Serving

Est. Active Time: 15 mins

Est. Total Time: 25 mins

Ingredients

- 1 tablespoon olive oil
- 1 cup canned no-salt-added chickpeas (garbanzo beans), rinsed and patted dry
- ½ teaspoon paprika
- ¼ teaspoon garlic powder
- ¼ teaspoon ground cumin
- ⅛ teaspoon ground pepper
- 2 cups Roasted Butternut Squash & Root Vegetables

- 1 1/3 cups Lemon-Roasted Mixed Vegetables
- 1 cup fresh baby spinach
- ½ cup cherry tomatoes, halved
- ¼ cup crumbled reduced-fat feta cheese (1 oz.)
- 2 (6 to 7 inch) whole-wheat pita bread rounds, halved horizontally and lightly toasted
- ½ cup hummus
- Lemon wedges

Instructions

- In a 10-inch skillet set over medium heat, heat the oil. Add chickpeas and season with pepper, paprika, cumin, and garlic powder. Cook the chickpeas for 6 to 8 minutes while stirring frequently until they are lightly browned.

- The chickpeas should be moved to a medium bowl. Add Lemon-Roasted Mixed Vegetables, Roasted Butternut Squash & Root Vegetables, spinach, tomatoes, and feta; gently toss to combine. Serve with lemon wedges, pita, and hummus.

Stuffed Sweet Potatoes with Chili

Servings : 4

20.1 grams Protein

26.8 grams Carb

9.1 grams Fat

266 Cal Per Serving

Est. Active Time: 15 mins

Est. Total Time: 25 mins

Ingredients

- 2 small sweet potatoes (about 8 oz. each)
- 1 tablespoon canola oil
- 8 ounces 95%-lean ground beef
- 2 scallions, sliced, green and white parts separated
- 2 tablespoons tomato paste
- 1-2 canned chipotle peppers in adobo, chopped
- 1 tablespoon paprika
- ¼ teaspoon salt

- 1 cup canned low-sodium kidney beans, rinsed
- ½ cup water
- ¼ cup shredded Mexican-blend cheese
- 4 teaspoons reduced-fat sour cream for garnish

Instructions

- Set the oven to 425 degrees Fahrenheit. A baking sheet should be foil-lined.
- Place the sweet potatoes on the prepared pan after giving them several fork pricks. Bake for 40 to 45 minutes, or until a knife inserted comes out clean. Allow to cool a bit.
- Oil should be heated in a big skillet while doing this. Add ground beef and the whites of the scallions. Cook the beef, stirring and breaking it up with a wooden spoon, for about 4 minutes, or until it is

no longer pink. Add salt, paprika, chipotles, and tomato paste as desired. About 1 minute, while stirring, cook the tomato paste until it starts to brown. Cook, stirring, the water and beans mixture for another minute or more, or until the majority of the liquid has evaporated. Cover up to stay warm.

- The sweet potatoes should be cut in half lengthwise. Scoop the flesh into a medium bowl while preserving the skins. Stir in 1 cup of the chili mixture after adding it. Place the sweet potato-chili mixture inside each potato skin (the skins will be full). Re-add the cheese and remaining chili mixture to the baking sheet.

- Bake for 3 to 5 minutes, or until the cheese is melted and the potatoes are well heated. If desired, add sour cream as a garnish and top with scallion greens.

Chopped   Salad   with   Chicken   &
Avocado-Buttermilk Dressing

Servings : 4

29.7 grams Protein

27.9 grams Carb

13 grams Fat

337 Cal Per Serving

Est. Active Time: 20 mins

Est. Total Time: 20 mins

Ingredients

- 1 cup buttermilk
- ½ ripe avocado
- 3 tablespoons chopped fresh herbs, such as tarragon, mint and/or parsley
- 1 tablespoon rice vinegar
- ¾ teaspoon salt
- ½ teaspoon ground pepper
- 4 cups chopped kale
- 2 cups shredded red cabbage
- 2 cups broccoli florets, finely chopped

- 2 cups shredded cooked chicken
- 1 cup shredded carrots
- ½ cup finely chopped red onion
- ½ cup toasted sliced almonds
- ⅓ cup dried cherries or cranberries

Instructions

- Blenderized ingredients include buttermilk, avocado, herbs, vinegar, salt, and pepper.
- In a big bowl, mix together the kale, cabbage, broccoli, chicken, carrots, onion, almonds, and cherries (or cranberries). Re-toss after adding the dressing.

Lentil Stew with Salsa Verde

Servings : 4

18.8 grams Protein

53.1 grams Carb

5.2 grams Fat

322 Cal Per Serving

Est. Active Time: 30 mins

Est. Total Time: 40 mins

Ingredients

- 1 tablespoon olive oil
- 1 ¼ cups finely chopped celery (4-6 stalks) or fennel (1 bulb)
- 3 small carrots, peeled and finely chopped (1/2 cup)
- ½ cup finely chopped red bell pepper
- 5 tablespoons finely chopped shallot (1 large), divided
- 2 large cloves garlic, minced
- 2 tablespoons tomato paste

- 1 ½ cups French green lentils, sorted and rinsed
- 4 cups low-sodium chicken broth or vegetable broth, or water
- ¾ teaspoon ground pepper, divided
- ½ teaspoon salt, divided
- 1 small bunch Italian parsley, finely chopped (about 3/4 cup)
- 1 large lime, juiced (2 Tbsp.)
- 2 tablespoons white-wine vinegar

Instructions

- In a 4- to 6-qt pot, heat the oil over medium-high heat. Add the carrots, bell pepper, 3 tablespoons of shallot, and the garlic. Cook for about 3 minutes while stirring until softened. Cook for 30 seconds while stirring in the tomato paste. Add the lentils, water or broth, 1/2 teaspoon of pepper, and 1/4 teaspoon of salt. up to a boil. For 35 to 40 minutes, or until the lentils are tender, cover the pot, lower the heat, and simmer.

- In the meantime, combine the remaining 2 Tbsp. shallot, lime juice, vinegar, 1/4 tsp. salt, and pepper in a small bowl; stir well.

- Divide the stew among 4 bowls and spoon salsa verde on top of each to serve. Separately distribute the remaining salsa verde.

Forbidden Rice & White Kimchi Steak Salad

Servings :4

20.5 grams Protein

36.5 grams Carb

32.2 grams Fat

495 Cal Per Serving

Est. Active Time: 45 mins

Est. Total Time: 60 mins

Ingredients

- 8 ounces hanger or boneless rib-eye steak, trimmed
- ¾ teaspoon salt, divided
- ¾ cup plus 2 tablespoons water
- ½ cup forbidden rice or brown rice
- 5 tablespoons extra-virgin olive oil, divided, plus more to taste
- 1 cup thinly sliced shallots
- 2 cups sliced shiitake mushrooms

- 4 scallions, trimmed and cut into 1/2-inch pieces
- 1 large ripe avocado, cubed
- ½ cup white kimchi (baek kimchi) or fresh sauerkraut, drained
- 4 cups tatsoi, spinach or other tender greens
- 1 tablespoon lemon juice
- ¼ cup toasted sunflower seeds

Instructions

- Steak should be salted with 1/4 teaspoon and left to rest for 30 minutes or up to a day in the refrigerator.
- In a tiny pan, bring water to a boil. Cook rice for 30 to 40 minutes for brown rice or 30 to 40 minutes for prohibited rice, stirring occasionally, until water is just barely absorbed. Spread the rice out on a

baking sheet to cool after adding 1 tablespoon oil and 1/4 teaspoon salt.

- Shale slices should be cut into rings in the interim. A medium skillet with 3 tablespoons oil is heated to medium. Add the shallots and cook, stirring frequently, for 6 to 8 minutes, or until browned and crispy. Transfer the shallots to a plate with a slotted spoon and set aside.

- 1/8 teaspoon salt and mushrooms should be added to the pan. Cook for about 5 minutes while stirring occasionally. Scallions should be added and cooked for about a minute while stirring. Place in a sizable bowl.

- To the pan, add the last tablespoon of oil. Cook the steak for 3 to 4 minutes on each side, turning it once, and adjusting the heat as needed, until it is browned and an instant-read thermometer inserted in the thickest section reads 135 degrees F. Place on a fresh cutting board and set aside to rest for ten minutes. Cube the food.

- Transfer the rice to the bowl containing the vegetables, then top with the steak, avocado, kimchi, or sauerkraut. Gently stir to combine. Divide between four small dishes.

- Greens should be added to the large bowl along with the remaining 1/8 teaspoon of salt and lemon juice. Add the greens, the saved shallots, and the sunflower seeds on top of the rice mixture. Adding more oil is optional.

Chili-Rubbed Chicken with Coconut Rice & Mango Salsa

Servings :4

29.4 grams Protein

50.4 grams Carb

17.9 grams Fat

478 Cal Per Serving

Est. Active Time: 20 mins

Est. Total Time: 55 mins

Ingredients

- 1 (14 ounce) can light coconut milk
- ⅔ cup short-grain brown rice
- ¾ teaspoon salt, divided
- 2 tablespoons extra-virgin olive oil, divided
- 1 teaspoon chili powder
- 1 clove garlic, grated
- 1 pound boneless, skinless chicken breast
- 1 large mango, diced
- 1 medium red bell pepper, diced

- ½ medium red onion, diced
- ¼ cup chopped fresh cilantro
- 3 tablespoons lime juice

Instructions

- Set oven to 400 degrees Fahrenheit.
- Rice, coconut milk, and 1/4 teaspoon salt are all mixed together in a medium saucepan. Heat to a rolling boil over medium-high. Cook the rice for about 45 minutes, stirring occasionally, until it is tender and the liquid has been absorbed.
- In the meantime, add 1 tablespoon oil, 1/4 teaspoon salt, chili powder, and garlic in a small bowl. On a baking sheet with a rim, arrange the chicken and massage with the spice mixture. Bake for about 20 minutes, flipping once, or until an instant-read thermometer inserted in the

thickest part reads 165 degrees F. Slice or chop after 15 minutes of resting.

- In a medium bowl, mix the mango, remaining 1 tablespoon oil, 1/4 teaspoon salt, bell pepper, onion, cilantro, and lime juice. Rice should be served with the chicken and salsa.

Feta & Roasted Red Pepper Stuffed Chicken Breast

Servings : 8

24.4 grams Protein

1.9 grams Carb

7.4 grams Fat

179 Cal Per Serving

Est. Active Time: 25 mins

Est. Total Time: 60 mins

Ingredients

- ½ cup crumbled feta cheese
- ½ cup chopped roasted red bell peppers
- ½ cup chopped fresh spinach
- ¼ cup Kalamata olives, pitted and quartered
- 1 tablespoon chopped fresh basil
- 1 tablespoon chopped fresh flat-leaf parsley
- 2 cloves garlic, minced

- 4 (8 ounce) boneless, skinless chicken breasts
- ¼ teaspoon salt
- ½ teaspoon ground pepper
- 1 tablespoon extra-virgin olive oil
- 1 tablespoon lemon juice

Instructions

- Set the oven to 400 °F. In a medium bowl, combine the feta, spinach, olives, basil, parsley, and garlic.
- Create a pocket by making a horizontal slit through the thickest part of each chicken breast with a small knife. Fill each breast pocket with about 1/3 cup of the feta mixture, and then use wooden picks to keep the pockets closed. Salt and pepper should be uniformly distributed on the chicken.

- In a sizable oven-safe skillet, heat oil over medium-high heat. Place the stuffed breasts in the pan with the tops facing down and cook for 2 minutes or until golden. Flip the chicken carefully, then place the pan in the oven. Bake for 20 to 25 minutes, or until an instant-read thermometer inserted in the thickest part of the chicken reads 165°F.
- Lemon juice should be applied evenly to the chicken. Before serving, take the wooden picks out of the chicken.

Roasted Salmon with Spicy Cranberry Relish

Servings : 8

28.6 grams Protein

7.6 grams Carb

8.8 grams Fat

229 Cal Per Serving

Est. Active Time: 80 mins

Est. Total Time: 80 mins

Ingredients

- 2 ½ pounds skin-on salmon fillet
- 2 cloves garlic, peeled and chopped
- 1 ½ teaspoons kosher salt, divided
- ½ teaspoon whole black peppercorns, cracked
- 1 lemon, zested and cut into wedges
- 2 tablespoons extra-virgin olive oil, divided
- 2 teaspoons Dijon mustard

- 2 cups cranberries, fresh or frozen (8 ounces)
- 1 small shallot, minced
- 1 serrano pepper, seeded
- 1 medium Granny Smith apple, peeled and finely diced
- 1 stalk celery, finely diced
- 1 tablespoon balsamic vinegar
- 2 tablespoons chopped fresh parsley, divided

Instructions

- Set oven to 400 degrees Fahrenheit. Use parchment paper to line a baking sheet with a rim.
- Salmon should be put on the prepared pan. Use a fork or a mortar and pestle to mash the garlic, 1 teaspoon of salt, peppercorns, and lemon zest into a paste. Add 1 tablespoon oil and mustard after

being transferred to a small bowl. smother the salmon with. Bake for 10 to 15 minutes, or until the meat flakes readily with a fork.

- Cranberries, shallot, and serrano are chopped into a fine powder in the meantime using a food processor. Add apple, celery, vinegar, 1 tablespoon parsley, the remaining 1 tablespoon oil, and 1/2 teaspoon salt to the medium bowl after transferring.

- Along with the relish and lemon wedges, top the salmon with the final 1 tablespoon of parsley.

Chicken Hummus Bowl

Servings : 4

31.1 grams Protein

27.3 grams Carb

29.4 grams Fat

485 Cal Per Serving

Est. Active Time: 25 mins

Est. Total Time: 25 mins

Ingredients

- 1 pound boneless, skinless chicken thighs, trimmed and cut into 1-inch pieces
- 3 tablespoons extra-virgin olive oil, divided
- 1 teaspoon ground cumin
- 1 teaspoon paprika
- ¼ teaspoon cayenne pepper
- ¼ teaspoon salt, divided
- 2 cloves garlic, finely chopped

- 2 tablespoons lemon juice
- 2 cups hummus
- 1 Aleppo pepper, plus more for serving
- 1 pint cherry tomatoes, halved
- ¼ cup slivered red onion
- ¼ cup chopped fresh parsley

Instructions

- Place the rack in the upper third of the oven and turn the broiler to high. Use foil to cover a baking sheet with a rim.
- Toss chicken with 1 tablespoon oil, 1/8 teaspoon salt, cumin, paprika, and cayenne. On the preheated pan, spread evenly. 5 to 7 minutes under the broiler, or until almost done.
- In the meantime, use a fork to mash the garlic and the remaining 1/8 teaspoon salt into a paste. Whisk in the remaining 2 tablespoons of oil and lemon juice after

transferring to a medium bowl. Stirring occasionally, add the chicken and let stand for 5 minutes.

- Divide the hummus among 4 small plates or bowls. Add the chicken, any leftover dressing, cucumber, tomato, onion, and parsley to the plate.

Linguine with Creamy Mushroom Sauce

Servings : 4

16.5 grams Protein

58.9 grams Carb

18.2 grams Fat

479 Cal Per Serving

Est. Active Time: 40 mins

Est. Total Time: 40 mins

Ingredients

- 8 ounces whole-wheat linguine pasta
- 2 tablespoons extra-virgin olive oil
- 6 cloves garlic, sliced
- 1 ½ pounds mixed mushrooms, sliced
- 1 cup diced shallots
- 1 tablespoon chopped fresh thyme
- 1 cup dry white wine
- ½ cup sour cream or crème fraîche
- ¼ cup grated Parmesan cheese plus more for garnish

- 1 tablespoon butter
- ½ teaspoon salt
- ¼ teaspoon ground pepper
- Finely chopped fresh parsley for garnish

Instructions

- Over high heat, bring a sizable pot of water to a boil. As directed on the package, cook the pasta. After draining the pasta, save 1/2 cup of the water.

- In the meantime, in a large skillet, heat the oil and garlic over medium heat until fragrant, about 2 minutes. Turn up the heat to high and stir in the mushrooms, shallots, and thyme. Cook, occasionally stirring, for 11 to 13 minutes, or until the liquid the mushrooms release has evaporated and the mushrooms are beginning to brown.

- Cook the wine in the pan for 3 minutes, or until it has reduced by about half. Add the sour cream (or crème fraîche), Parmesan, butter, salt, and pepper to the pasta along with the reserved pasta water. Pasta is added, then it is coated. Add more Parmesan and parsley to serve.

Pizza-Stuffed Spaghetti Squash

Servings : 4

16.4 grams Protein

32.2 grams Carb

20.6 grams Fat

373 Cal Per Serving

Est. Active Time: 50 mins

Est. Total Time: 60 mins

Ingredients

- 1 (2 1/2 to 3 pound) spaghetti squash, halved lengthwise and seeded
- ¼ cup water
- 2 tablespoons extra-virgin olive oil
- 1 cup chopped onion
- 2 large cloves garlic, minced
- 1 (8 ounce) package mushrooms, sliced
- 1 cup chopped bell pepper (any color)
- 2 cups no-salt-added crushed tomatoes
- 1 teaspoon Italian seasoning

- ½ teaspoon ground pepper, divided
- ¼ teaspoon crushed red pepper
- ¼ teaspoon salt, divided
- 2 ounces pepperoni, halved, divided
- 1 cup shredded part-skim mozzarella cheese, divided
- 2 tablespoons grated Parmesan cheese

Instructions

- Place the oven rack in the upper third and heat it to 450 degrees F.
- Squash halves should be placed cut-side down in a microwave-safe dish with water. 10–12 minutes on High, uncovered, until the flesh is soft. (An alternative is to arrange the squash cut-side down on a sizable baking sheet with a rim. Bake for 40 to 50 minutes at 400°F until tender.)

- In the interim, warm the oil in a big skillet over medium heat. Add the onion and garlic; stir-fry for 3 to 4 minutes, or until the onion is beginning to soften. Cook, stirring, the bell pepper and mushrooms for a further five minutes or until the vegetables are soft. Tomatoes, Italian seasoning, 1/4 tsp. pepper, crushed red pepper, and 1/8 tsp. salt should all be added.
- Cook for 2 minutes, or until the food is thoroughly heated and the flavors are unified. With the exception of 10 or 12 pepperoni halves, remove from heat and stir in. Cover and hold.
- Scrape the squash from the shells into a sizable bowl using a fork, being careful to preserve the shells. Add the remaining 1/4 teaspoon pepper, 1/8 teaspoon salt, and 1/4 cup mozzarella. Mix thoroughly

to coat the basin before adding the tomato mixture. Put the squash shells on a rimmed baking sheet, cut-side up. Separate the filling into the two halves. Then, sprinkle the remaining 3/4 cup mozzarella over the top and add the reserved pepperoni.

- Bake for about 15 minutes, or until the cheese is melted and the filling is heated.
- Turn the broiler to high and broil, carefully watching, for 1 to 2 minutes, or until the cheese and pepperoni start to brown. To serve, divide each boat in half.

Salmon Caesar Salad

Servings : 4

34.8 grams Protein

7.9 grams Carb

12.8 grams Fat

291 Cal Per Serving

Est. Active Time: 20 mins

Est. Total Time: 20 mins

Ingredients

- 1 ½ tablespoons extra-virgin olive oil
- 4 (5 ounce) skinless salmon fillets
- 1 teaspoon ground pepper, divided
- ⅛ teaspoon salt plus 1/2 teaspoon, divided
- ½ cup buttermilk
- ¼ cup nonfat plain Greek yogurt
- ¼ cup grated Parmigiano-Reggiano cheese
- 2 tablespoons lemon juice

- 1 ½ teaspoons Worcestershire sauce
- 1 teaspoon grated garlic
- ½ teaspoon Dijon mustard
- 5 cups chopped romaine lettuce
- 3 cups chopped radicchio
- 3 tablespoons thinly sliced fresh basil, plus more for garnish
- 1 ½ tablespoons chopped fresh tarragon

Instructions

- In a sizable nonstick skillet, heat the oil over medium-high heat until it shimmers. Add 1/8 teaspoon salt and 1/2 teaspoon pepper to the salmon. Add the salmon to the pan and cook for 3 to 4 minutes on each side, or until it is golden brown and flakes easily with a fork. Break into big chunks and transfer to a platter.
- In a big bowl, combine buttermilk, yogurt, cheese, lemon juice,

Worcestershire, garlic, mustard, and the last half teaspoon of each pepper and salt. In a small bowl, place 1/4 cup of the dressing aside. Toss the lettuce, radicchio, basil, and tarragon together in the big bowl.

- Place the salmon on top of the salad in a serving dish. Serve with additional basil and the 1/4 cup dressing you saved.

Caprese Turkey Burgers

Servings : 4

33.3 grams Protein

24.8 grams Carb

27.5 grams Fat

472 Cal Per Serving

Est. Active Time: 30 mins

Est. Total Time: 30 mins

Ingredients

- 1 pound lean ground turkey
- 1 teaspoon Italian seasoning
- ½ teaspoon garlic powder
- ¼ teaspoon salt
- ¼ teaspoon ground pepper
- ¼ teaspoon crushed red pepper
- 1 tablespoon extra-virgin olive oil
- 4 ounces fresh mozzarella, sliced into 4 pieces
- ¼ cup mayonnaise

- ¼ cup chopped basil plus 1/3 cup basil leaves, divided
- 8 slices tomato (from 2 tomatoes)
- 1 teaspoon balsamic vinegar
- 4 whole-wheat buns, toasted

Instructions

- In a medium bowl, mix the turkey with the Italian seasoning, garlic powder, salt, pepper, and crushed red pepper. Make four equal patties with a diameter of about 4 inches.
- In a sizable nonstick skillet, heat the oil over medium-high heat. Burgers are added once heat is reduced to medium. For 4 minutes, cook. After turning over, add a slice of mozzarella to each. For an additional 3 to 4 minutes, cook with the cover off until an instant-read thermometer registers 165 degrees F.

- In the meantime, combine mayonnaise and basil leaves in a small bowl. On a plate, arrange tomato slices and drizzle with vinegar.
- Each bun's bottom should have about 1 tablespoon of the mayonnaise mixture spread on it. Burger, two tomato slices, and basil leaves should be placed on top.

Grilled Flank Steak with Tomato Salad

Servings : 4

25.3 grams Protein

3.9 grams Carb

25.1 grams Fat

346 Cal Per Serving

Est. Active Time: 10 mins

Est. Total Time: 20 mins

Ingredients

- 1 pint grape tomatoes, halved
- ½ cup chopped fresh cilantro
- ⅓ cup extra-virgin olive oil
- 1 small jalapeño pepper, seeded and sliced
- 2 teaspoons finely chopped garlic
- ½ teaspoon salt, divided
- 1 1-pound flank steak
- ½ teaspoon ground pepper

Instructions

- Set the grill to medium-high heat or preheat the grill pan.
- In a medium bowl, mix the tomatoes, cilantro, oil, jalapenos, garlic, and 1/4 teaspoon salt.
- Add the final 1/4 teaspoon of salt and pepper to the meat. Grill for 3 to 5 minutes on each side or until an instant-read thermometer inserted in the center registers 125 degrees F for medium-rare.
- Slice the steak thinly across the grain on a clean cutting board, preferably one with grooves for catching juices. Four plates should receive the slices. Top the steak with the tomato salad and any juices that have accumulated on the cutting board.

Shrimp Cauliflower Fried Rice

Servings : 4

30.1 grams Protein

9.6 grams Carb

16.9 grams Fat

309 Cal Per Serving

Est. Active Time: 25 mins

Est. Total Time: 25 mins

Ingredients

- ¼ cup sesame oil, divided
- 2 large eggs, lightly beaten
- 3 cups riced cauliflower
- 1 pound large shrimp (31-35 count), peeled and deveined
- 3 cups broccoli florets
- 1 medium red bell pepper, thinly sliced (about 1 cup)
- 3 cloves garlic, sliced

- 3 tablespoons reduced-sodium soy sauce or tamari
- 2 tablespoons water
- 1 tablespoon rice vinegar
- ½ teaspoon ground pepper

Instructions

- In a large, heavy skillet or wok with a flat bottom made of carbon steel, heat 2 tablespoons of oil over high heat. Add the eggs and cook them for about 30 seconds, flipping them only once, without stirring. About 15 seconds after flipping, fry the other side until just done. Cut into 1/2-inch pieces after transferring to a cutting board.
- Heat the pan on a high heat while adding 2 teaspoons of oil. Cauliflower should be added in an equal layer; cook 3 to 4

minutes, stirring occasionally, until gently browned. Place on a plate.

- Heat the pan on a high heat while adding 2 teaspoons of oil. Add the shrimp; cook, tossing frequently, for about 3 minutes, or until just opaque. Place on the same platter as the cauliflower.

- Over high heat, add the remaining 2 tablespoons of oil to the pan. Add the broccoli, bell pepper, and garlic; simmer for 4 to 5 minutes, stirring periodically, until the broccoli is gently browned. Add pepper, vinegar, water, soy sauce (or tamari), and to taste. Boil for 30 seconds after bringing to a boil. Get rid of the heat. Add the shrimp, cauliflower, and eggs that were set aside.

Grilled Creole-Style Jambalaya

Servings : 4

26.8 grams Protein

53.7 grams Carb

19 grams Fat

504 Cal Per Serving

Est. Active Time: 45 mins

Est. Total Time: 60 mins

Ingredients

- 3 tablespoons canola oil, divided
- 1 cup long-grain brown rice
- 1 ¾ cups water
- 8 ounces andouille sausage, sliced 1/2 inch thick
- 8 ounces peeled and deveined raw shrimp (21-25 per pound)
- 1 medium green bell pepper, cut into 2-inch pieces
- 1 large red onion, cut into 2-inch pieces

- 8 ounces okra
- 2 ½ teaspoons Cajun seasoning, divided
- 1 ¼ teaspoons celery seed, divided
- ¾ teaspoon ground pepper, divided
- 1 large tomato, cored and cut in half
- Sliced scallions for garnish

Instructions

- Set the grill to medium-high heat.
- In a medium saucepan over medium-high heat, warm 1 tablespoon of oil. Add the rice and heat for 2 minutes, stirring regularly, until toasted. Add water, then turn down the heat so that it simmers. For 40 to 45 minutes, cook under cover to achieve tenderness.
- In the meantime, skewer the okra, bell pepper, onion, sausage, shrimp, and bell pepper separately. Sprinkle with 2 teaspoons Cajun seasoning, 1 teaspoon

celery seed, and 1/2 teaspoon pepper before adding the final 2 tablespoons of oil. Turning frequently, grill the skewers with the tomato halves and vegetables for 5 to 10 minutes, or until the shrimp are opaque and the sausage and vegetables are lightly charred.

- To keep warm, take the shrimp, sausage, and vegetables off the skewers and place them on a plate.

- Add the chopped tomato, the remaining 1/2 teaspoon of Cajun seasoning, and 1/4 teaspoons of celery seed and pepper to the cooked rice. On a serving tray, spread the rice, then add the shrimp, sausage, and vegetables. If desired, top with scallions.

Cochinita Pibil (Yucatán-Style Pulled Pork)

Servings : 6

49.4 grams Protein

29.8 grams Carb

16.6 grams Fat

472 Cal Per Serving

Est. Active Time: 60 mins

Est. Total Time: 120 mins

Ingredients

- 2 ½ tablespoons Annatto Spice Blend
- 2 ½ tablespoons cider vinegar
- 2 tablespoons orange juice
- 1 tablespoon lime juice
- 3 cloves garlic, grated
- 1 ½ teaspoons kosher salt
- 2 ¼ pounds boneless pork shoulder, trimmed and cut into 2-inch pieces
- 2 pieces banana leaves, 10 by 10 inches each, thawed if frozen

- 1 cup water
- ½ medium red onion, very thinly sliced
- 2 ¼ cups water, divided
- 2 habanero or red jalapeño peppers, halved, seeded and thinly sliced
- ½ cup cider vinegar
- 3 whole cloves or 4 allspice berries
- ½ teaspoon dried Mexican oregano
- ¼ teaspoon whole black peppercorns
- ¾ teaspoon kosher salt
- 12 (6 inch) corn tortillas, warmed
- Cotija cheese & lime wedges for serving

Instructions

- Pork preparation: In a big bowl, mix together the spice mixture, 2 1/2 tablespoons vinegar, orange juice, lime juice, garlic, and 1 1/2 teaspoons salt. Stir in the pork to coat.

- Trim any sharp, brown edges and rinse off any white residue if using banana leaves. In a 6-qt. electric pressure cooker, arrange one leaf so that it completely covers the bottom of the inner pot. (Or, view the oven variation.) Place the pork in a single layer and top with any remaining bowl juices. Around the meat, pour one cup of water. Wrap in the opposite banana leaf. (If not using banana leaves, continue with setting up the meat and adding the water without them.)
- Cook for 45 minutes at high pressure with the lid locked on.
- Pickled onion and pepper preparation in the interim: In a compact, deep heatproof bowl, put the onion. Add two cups of water, cover, and leave for ten minutes.

Return to the bowl after a thorough drain. Include peppers.

- In a small saucepan, mix the remaining 1/4 cup water, vinegar, cloves (or allspice), oregano, peppercorns, and salt. Over a high heat, bring to a lively simmer, then pour over the vegetables. Stirring occasionally, set aside.

- Allow the pressure in the cooker to naturally relax for 15 minutes. Manually release any remaining pressure after unlocking and removing the lid. To remove the banana leaves, use tongs.

- With two forks, shred the pork after transferring it to a serving plate. To keep warm, loosely cover with a banana leaf or foil.

- Cooking liquid should be poured into a measuring cup and left for 10 minutes. Skim off any fat. Put the liquid back in the pot, switch the stove on Saute, and then bring to a boil. Cook for 5 to 7 minutes, or until reduced by half. Pork and liquid should be combined.

- Vegetables are drained, and entire spices are taken out. If preferred, top the tortilla-wrapped meat and vegetables with crumbled cotija and wedges of lime.

Volume Conversions

Cup	Ounce	Milliliter	TableSpoon
8 Cup	64 oz	1895 ml	128
6 Cup	48 oz	1420 ml	96
5 Cup	40 oz	1180 ml	80
4 Cup	32 oz	960 ml	64
2 Cup	16 oz	480 ml	32
1 Cup	8 oz	240 ml	16
¾ Cup	6 oz	177 ml	12
⅔ Cup	5 oz	158 ml	11
½ Cup	4 oz	118ml	8
⅜ Cup	3 oz	90 ml	6
⅓ Cup	2.5 oz	79 ml	5.5

¼ Cup	2 oz	59 ml	4
⅛ Cup	1 oz	30 ml	3
1/16 Cup	½ oz	15 ml	1

Fahrenheit	Celsius
100	37
150	65
200	93
250	121
300	150
325	160
350	180
375	190
400	200
435	220
450	230
500	260
525	274
550	288

Weight Conversion

Imperial	Metric
½oz	15g
1oz	29g
2oz	57g
3oz	85g
4oz	113g
5oz	141g
6oz	170g
8oz	227g
10oz	283g
12oz	340g
13oz	369g

14oz	397g
15oz	425g
1lb	453g

1 tablespoon = 3 teaspoons = 15 milliliters

4 tablespoons = 1/4 cup = 60 milliliters

1 ounce = 2 tablespoons = 30 milliliters

1 cup = 8 oz. = 250 milliliters

1 pint = 2 cups = 500 milliliters

1 quart = 4 cups = 950 milliliters

1 quart = 2 pints = 950 milliliters

1 gallon = 4 quarts = 3800 milliliters = 3.8 liters

Made in the USA
Las Vegas, NV
01 February 2024

85167935R00118